REVELATION IN JEWISH
WISDOM LITERATURE

REVELATION IN JEWISH
WISDOM LITERATURE

By J. COERT RYLAARSDAM

THE UNIVERSITY OF CHICAGO PRESS
CHICAGO · ILLINOIS

L. C. # A 46 - 3156

THE UNIVERSITY OF CHICAGO PRESS, CHICAGO 37

Copyright 1946 by The University of Chicago. All rights reserved
Published 1946. Second Impression 1951. Composed and printed by
THE UNIVERSITY OF CHICAGO PRESS, *Chicago, Illinois, U.S.A.*

Midway Reprint 1974

INTRODUCTION

IN CHRISTIAN life and thought some problems are perennial. From time to time they reappear in altered dress, and their apparent insistence varies; but, whether slumbering or active, they are always present. One of them is the question of authority, involving the tension between unity and freedom. Some point to the Bible as authority, the touchstone for ideas and deeds. They are immediately reminded that all who agree with them are not of one mind about the thought and life inculcated by the Bible. Those reminding them may refer them to some standard interpretation of the Bible on these points, some creed or confession. But soon it becomes clear that this authoritative "statement" also needs its interpreters. At this point the seeker for authority may be introduced to a church which claims to function as an authoritative agency of interpretations; but examination invariably shows that its claims rest on its own interpretation of the Bible, of which it claims to be the true custodian. An individual is torn between the urge to "belong" to some group claiming external authority by giving assent to its deliverances and the desire to answer for himself, by means of his own faculties, the unbidden questions and challenges that the experience of living throws up. Where and what is the ultimate norm?

Another question perennially present in the history of Christian life and thought is spoken of as the problem of nature and grace. Does the human mind, in its exercise of freedom and in its capacity for observation, experimentation, and analysis, discover the true way of life? Granting that there is a God who creates men, is the divine act of creation, which endows them with a reasoning and purposive consciousness, the only "grace" God grants them? Or are men, at least some of them, given special aid over and above this "natural" endowment? If so, in what manner or form is it given, and how is it related to the natural urge for understanding? Does it supplement nature? Or does it deny its validity?

We note that the two ever recurrent problems cited above are closely interrelated. If knowledge of the way of life is to be found solely through the rise of the natural human mind, then the problem of authority, in a practical sense at least, is largely a social one. But if, on the other hand, aid or grace of a special nature is given men over and beyond their natural creaturely endowments, then the problem of authority, also in a practical sense, is theological as well as social. Its social aspect will be determined very largely by the manner and form in which it is asserted that the special aid manifests itself. Both questions are thus involved in a consideration of the problem of revelation, i.e., the manner and means in and by which men come to possess a knowledge both of the true goals of life and of the way by which they can attain them. A growing tendency to begin the study of theology empirically and experimentally through the discipline afforded by the social sciences and, at the other extreme, the strongly irrational and transcendental element implicit in the theological movement popularly known as "Barthianism" have made this problem seem very central in recent years. The gap becomes so wide that the tension between human and divine activity, historically present in considerations of the problem of revelation, tends to snap. "Humanism" and "supernaturalism" are sometimes set over against each other in such a manner as to deny to both at least some legitimate place in a larger whole which recognizes both human creaturehood and human freedom.

The study of the Hebrew Wisdom Literature here presented introduces the problems of revelation and, consequently, of authority and grace from a historical and biblical point of view. The books of Proverbs, Job, and Ecclesiastes in the canon and the books of the Wisdom of Jesus ben Sira, the Wisdom of Solomon, Baruch, IV Maccabees, and the Pirke Aboth of the extra-canonical literature are the chief documents. This literature of the wisdom movement is much less well known than either the legal or the prophetic aspects of Hebrew cultural and religious development. The possible reasons for this comparative ignorance are various. Only part of the literature is in the canon of Scripture. Most of it is of a nonnarrative character. It is didactic, prudential, and philosophical. With the exception of the Wisdom of Solomon and IV Maccabees, it is somewhat lacking in a passionately religious note that calls for "decisions" and obedience. Rather, it busies itself with a discussion of life's relationships. Too often, perhaps, the documents making up the wisdom corpus have been studied as separate units, illustrative of Hebrew literary genius or prudential acuteness rather than as integral and related parts of a mosaic illustrative of a view of life constantly in process of development.

As we have already intimated, our study owes its inception to the urgent questions about authority and grace in current religious discussion. Inasmuch as Christianity is rooted in the Bible, it seems pertinent to refer to it for an understanding of the genesis of these ever present problems. But how did we come to select the Wisdom Literature as our particular area of biblical study? The reason is the very close connection between the terms "spirit" and "wisdom" as instruments and evidences of revelation. We have dealt in some detail with this identification in our final chapter, suggesting its significance for New Testament and Christian ideas about revelation. The connection was first noted in the New Testament, where we began our inquiry into biblical views of revelation by a cursory analysis of the role played by the spirit. Wisdom and spirit were identified with each other, and both were equated with the glorified Jesus.

This identification of wisdom and spirit seemed to intimate that the roots for Christian ideas about revelation go through the New Testament back into the Old Testament, and perhaps especially into the Wisdom Literature. Any study of the question in the New Testament would have to be prefaced by a study of this material. And so, the limitations of time and space being what they are, this book ends with the completion of the preface of the project!

The Hebrew Wisdom Literature has its own peculiar place in the development of Jewish religion. In contrast to the prophetic and legal traditions, the movement which it records was consciously related to analogous movements both in Egypt and in Mesopotamia. Both of these antedated the Jewish movement. At its inception the Hebrew movement shows no religious or national particularism to inhibit its full correspondence with the more ancient traditions of wisdom in other lands. It may have arisen in imitation of

these, or it may have begun as a "revolt" of a free-thinking,
empirically minded element of "scientists" against the tribalistic and irrational ideas of religion characteristic of pre-
Exilic Hebrews. The later writings of the wisdom movement show that it returned to a full acceptance of the Jewish religious outlook. This may be accounted for by a growing sense of the significance of national peculiarity or by the
impact which the earlier free emphasis of wisdom had made
upon the whole religious outlook—a development somewhat analogous to the story of the conflict between science
and religion in Europe and America during the last century.

We have dealt with the history of the movement and
with its literary record only to enable us to grasp its basic
ideas. The central question has always been the problem of
revelation. How did the men who produced this literature
think that God and his ways became known to them? How
could men come by an understanding of the nature of life
that would enable them to see and attain its true significance? It soon becomes clear that the Wisdom Literature does
not offer a single, static reply to these questions. But it
likewise becomes apparent that the underlying unity for
all this material, superficially as divergent as Proverbs and
Job or as antithetical as Ecclesiastes and the Wisdom of
Solomon, is its preoccupation throughout, whether consciously or unconsciously, with the primary questions about
revelation to which we have addressed ourselves. The literature covers a period of about six centuries; yet all of it may
be considered as relevant to a single debate on this question.

The debate opens with an advocacy of personal freedom
and an employment of the natural human endowment of
mind and reason as the sufficient resources to attain an un-

derstanding of life. It closes with assertions that this understanding of life which is the attainment of wisdom is not
made possible by the unfettered human mind but by God's
special gift. This special gift is wisdom, the Law of the Jews,
or, as in the Wisdom of Solomon, the divine spirit. It is
granted only to some—that is, in classical theological terms
the movement begins with an emphasis upon the sufficiency
of nature, reason, creation, and it ends with an assertion of
the necessity of grace, faith, redemption. It opens in a spirit
of indifference toward the national cult, including the Law;
it closes in glorification of the cult and absorption by it.

Yet the transition from one extreme to the other is a
very gradual process. Neither "side" of the debate ever
wholly denies the other. They oppose each other but are
held in tension by the awareness that both rest on a common
foundation. The side emphatic about personal freedom and
reason is aware of its creaturehood and recognizes its natural powers as gifts of God; and the side emphatic about
special divine initiative never discounts the place of human
reason. There is wisdom in God and there is wisdom in man.
Both have spirit. The Hebrew wisdom movement throughout has a place for the divine image in which man was created, albeit not always equally spacious.

In presenting this modest study we wish to acknowledge
our debt to all who have aided in its preparation. Gratitude
is due especially to Professors John W. Beardslee, William
A. Irwin, and Ernest C. Colwell, all of whom in different
ways and at various stages gave assistance, without which
its completion and publication would not have been possible.

TABLE OF CONTENTS

CHAPTER I

THE CONTEXT OF HEBREW WISDOM

ISRAEL was a very young nation among the many peoples that produced the culture, or the cultures, of the ancient Near East. For a long time the Hebrews were strangers in their new land; but, as it became their home, they adopted many of its laws, some of which had originally come from the valley of Mesopotamia. They built a temple, which was largely modeled upon Phoenician and Egyptian forms.[1] The recently discovered Ras Shamra tablets have again shown in striking fashion how deeply their religious ceremonial was affected by the age-old cults and rituals of Palestine.[2] Israel, small as well as late, was touched by many streams of ancient life and took something from each. Because it was in vassalage to one great power after another, it was inevitable that it should borrow. By 1000 B.C. the Hebrews were still without an appreciable national literature, though in the valleys both of the Nile and of the Euphrates, as well as in Syria and among the peoples of the Crescent, the golden age of literary activity was over or on the wane. But this young nation had enormous powers of assimilation, and, under the aegis of its own peculiar genius, it was able further to develop what others had begun. This is also true of Israel's

[1] Millar Burrows, *What Mean These Stones?* (New Haven: American Schools of Oriental Research, 1941), p. 203.

[2] Claude F. A. Schaeffer, *Ugaritica: études relatives aux découvertes de Ras Shamra* (Paris: P. Geuthner, 1939), contains an excellent and complete bibliography.

1

Wisdom Literature, which, in its earliest forms, bore the fewest national characteristics of all Hebrew literature. Political and commercial contacts produce cultural and literary interdependence. By virtue of its geographic position the small land of Palestine was politically a bone of contention and commercially a land-bridge between the two great river cultures of the Nile and the Euphrates. Domination of the lands westward to the Mediterranean was the boast of all the great rulers of the first Babylonian Empire. The great trade route between Egypt and Mesopotamia came down from Damascus, entered Palestine just south of the Sea of Galilee, and crossed it westward and southward by way of Ashdod and Gaza. A Phoenician trade route united with this road in Palestine at Megiddo. And east of the Jordan the "King's Highway" united Syria with the Gulf of Akaba. The commerce and travel of all nations met and crossed in Palestine, making it a cosmopolitan center.

Mesopotamian influence in Palestine was very great. It began early. The mythologies of Palestine and Babylon were closely related. The Babylonian language and cuneiform writing remained in use in Palestine after the Egyptian conquest in 1479 B.C. and were actually employed by the Egyptian rulers in the composition of the Tell el-Amarna letters. Not infrequently, scribes from Palestine were employed in Egypt as teachers of Accadian writing. The language in Palestine always remained Semitic.

Following the Egyptian occupation of Palestine in the fifteenth century, political and commercial relations with that land remained close until the time of the Babylonian Exile. The generalization can be maintained that during the later period of the monarchy in Israel those who sought political security favored alliances with Mesopotamia, while those who sought rich economic benefits at the cost of political insecurity made up the pro-Egyptian party. Under Egyptian rule the sons of native vassals were educated at the Egyptian court.[3] Egyptian garrisons were stationed in Palestine in many places, introducing the culture and arts of the Nile and the worship of the Egyptian god Amon. Wen-Amon, who had come to the trade port of Byblos to procure cedar wood for a new temple, reported: "The fathers of the king of Byblos have sacrificed to Amon all their days."[4] Later the Phoenicians mediated much to Israel that they had first taken over from Egypt. In Gen. 43:11, balm, honey, gum, laudanum, and almonds are mentioned as exports to Egypt. Hosea 12:2 mentions the transport of oil, apparently as the price of an alliance. From Egypt came cloth, yarn, wheat, and precious objects (Gen. 42:7; Prov. 7:16; Dan. 11:42). Archeology has shown how deeply Egyptian products and culture influenced every aspect of life in Palestine.[5] Even after the establishment of an independent monarchy in Palestine, there is constant intercourse with Egypt and occasionally an invasion from that country. It seems almost inevitable that a people as expert as the Hebrews in cultural adaptation should have modeled some of their literary forms upon those current in Egypt.

Israel's Wisdom Literature well illustrates her use of the

[3] Hugo Gressmann, *Altorientalische Texte und Bilder zum Alten Testament*, Vol. I: *Altorientalische Texte zum Alten Testament* (Berlin: Walter de Gruyter & Co., 1926), p. 886: "Da führte man die Kinder der asiatischen Fürsten und ihre Brüder fort, um in den Festungen in Ägypten zu sein. Jedesmal aber, wenn einer von diesen Fürsten stirbt lasst seine Majestät dessen Sohn an seine Stelle treten."

[4] Alfred Bertholet, *A History of Hebrew Civilization*, trans. A. K. Dallas (London: George C. Harrap & Co., 1926), p. 85.

[5] Burrows, *op. cit.*, pp. 189–95, 200 f., 213 f., 217 f.

literary forms and subject matter current among the older cultures among which she grew up. This literature, whether in Egypt, Babylon, or Israel, divides itself into two kinds: prudential admonitions, commonly in proverbial form, that may serve the young as directions for a happy and successful life, and reflective essays on the meaning and significance of life, often in a pessimistic vein.

Egyptian wisdom materials now extant are quite voluminous. Among the prudential materials we include the Instructions of Ptahhotep, the Instruction of Kagemni, the Instruction of Duauf, the Instruction of King Amenemhet, and the Instructions for King Merikere. All these were originally written toward the end of the third and at the opening of the second millennium B.C.[6] They constitute the material for the instruction of the young men living at the court. In similar vein are two later documents: Papyrus Lansing, dated about 1100 B.C., and the Teaching of Amen-em-ope, dated anywhere from 1000 B.C. to 600 B.C.[7] Proverbs 22:17—23:10 are almost entirely made up of materials found in this book. Attempts have been made to show that the Egyptian document depended upon the Hebrew Book of Proverbs, conceivably possible if the Teaching of Amen-em-ope is placed as late as 600 B.C.[8] However, it is generally as-

[6] Adolf Erman, *The Literature of the Ancient Egyptians*, trans. Aylward M. Blackman (London: Methuen & Co., 1927), pp. 54 f.

[7] F. L. Griffith, "The Teaching of Amenophis, the Son of Kanekht: Papyrus B.M. 10474," *Journal of Egyptian Archaeology*, XII (1926), 226; W. O. E. Oesterley, *The Wisdom of Egypt and the Old Testament* (London: Society for the Propagation of the Gospel, 1927), pp. 9, 104 ff.; Ernest Budge, *The Teaching of Amen-em-apt, Son of Kanekht* (London: M. Hopkinson & Co., 1924), p. xi.

[8] Robert Oliver Kevin, "The Wisdom of Amen-em-apt and Its Possible Dependence upon the Hebrew Book of Proverbs," *Journal of the Society of Oriental Research*, XIV (1930), 115 ff.; cf. also James M. McGlinchey, *The Teaching of Amen-em-ope and*

sumed that in this instance, too, Israel was the borrower. Egyptian Wisdom Literature of the reflective type includes the Dispute with His Soul of One Who Is Tired of Life, the Admonitions of a Prophet, the Complaint of Khekheperre-Sonbu, and the Prophecy of Nefferohu. They originated in the last half of the third millenium B.C.[9]

Extant Wisdom Literature from Babylon is much more scanty than in the case of Egypt. The Babylonian Book of Proverbs, which employs the term "My son," so characteristic of the Hebrew Book of Proverbs, is alone as a sample of the prudential material. There are several documents of a reflective character, however: the Bilingual Book of Proverbs, the Babylonian Dialogue of Pessimism, and the Poem of the Righteous Sufferer, commonly known as "Babylonian Job."[10] It is very probable that the internationally famous Story of Ahikar also originated in Mesopotamia.[11] Its moral aphorisms may also be classified as part of the wisdom material of non-Hebrew origin.

Israel's Wisdom Literature is remarkably similar to that of Egypt and Babylon, though produced much later. Some of it is in the Old Testament canon: Proverbs, Job, Ecclesiastes, and some of the Psalms.[12] The Wisdom of Jesus ben Sira, I Esdras, Tobit, Baruch, and the Wisdom of Solomon are apocryphal documents that fall into the Wisdom Litera-

---

the Book of Proverbs (Washington: Catholic University of America Press, 1939); and Oesterley, op. cit., pp. 104 ff.

[9] Erman, op. cit., pp. 86 ff., 92 ff., 108 f., 110 f.

[10] Stephen Langdon, Babylonian Wisdom (London: Luzac & Co., 1923).

[11] R. H. Charles, The Apocrypha and Pseudepigrapha of the Old Testament in English (2 vols.; Oxford: Clarendon Press, 1913), II, 716.

[12] Especially Pss. 1, 19, 32, 34, 37, 49, 73, 94, 111, 112, 119, 127, 128, 133.

ture classification. We may further include the Letter of
Aristeas, IV Maccabees, and the Sayings of the Fathers
(Pirke Aboth). Of the early Christian literature, the Epistle
of James and the Didache have the closest affinity with Jewish wisdom materials.

The oldest collections of Hebrew wisdom are found in
the Book of Proverbs. By its own testimony this book is not
the work of a single author or collector. Further, chapters
1–9 differ radically from what follows. They are more speculative in outlook, and the literary forms are more complex
and developed. This is indicated by the fact that single
proverbs are tied together in larger unities and by the introduction of literary categories not strictly of the wisdom
type, such as the hymn.[13] These chapters are probably a
later introduction to the entire work. Gemser, however,
would date them before Ezra's work, since they lack all
traces of legalism.[14] Professor Pfeiffer dates the collections
of the book on the basis of what he terms their secular or
religious character, giving the earliest date to the collection
considered most secular. Thus he concludes that the following antedate the fifth century: 24:23–34 (D); chapters 25–27
(E¹); 30:1–10 (F¹); 30:11–33 (F²); 31:1–9 (G); and 31:10–
31 (H), the last-mentioned being the oldest. He feels that
the book as a whole must be dated after 400 B.C. to account
for the apparent references to the Law in 28:4, 9; the style
of chapters 1–9; and the personification of the concept of
wisdom in the eighth chapter.[15] There has been a strong

[13] B. Gemser, *Sprüche Salomos* (Tübingen: J. C. B. Mohr, 1937), p. 4.

[14] *Ibid.*, p. 5.

[15] Robert H. Pfeiffer, *Introduction to the Old Testament* (New York: Harper &
Bros., 1941), p. 659.

tendency in recent criticism to date the collections in chapters 10–29 in the pre-Exilic period. Thus Sellin assigns the nucleus of Prov. 10:1—22:16 to the time of Solomon and the beginnings of chapters 25–29 to the time of Hezekiah, 722–699 B.c.[16] The collections in 22:17—24:34, which include the materials also found in the Teaching of Amen-em-ope, he also places before the Exile. Hugo Gressmann places the earlier sections of Proverbs in the pre-prophetic period or at least in an era when the spirit of the Hebrew people was still young and when the viewpoint of its leaders had not yet been completely permeated by the prophetic outlook.[17] On the other hand, the assumption of many that in Israel the concept of individualism arose with the prophets Jeremiah and Ezekiel has caused some scholars to insist that the individualistic concern of the proverbial literature demands that it be dated later than these prophets of the seventh century.[18] The point is, however, that on any theory mentioned we must conclude that written records of Hebrew materials had scarcely begun at the time that the writing of the wisdom literature of surrounding peoples was drawing to a close. We have noted the possible exception in the case of the Teaching of Amen-em-ope, though even that seems unlikely. It is probable, then, that in all connections between the Hebrew and foreign wisdom materials Israel is the borrower.

That the Hebrews were familiar with the existence of

[16] Ernest Sellin, *Introduction to the Old Testament*, trans. W. Montgomery (New York: G. H. Doran, 1923), p. 209.

[17] *Israels Sprüchweisheit* (Berlin: Verlag Karl Curtius, 1925), pp. 34 f.

[18] Johannes Hempel, *Althebräische Literatur und ihre hellenistisch jüdisches Nachleben* (Wildpark-Potsdam: Akademische Verlag Gesellschaft, 1930), p. 55.

wisdom materials and activities beyond their own borders is abundantly clear from their own writings. Moreover, they imply that their wisdom was of the same genre. Solomon's wisdom was declared to be greater than that of Egypt or of all the sons of the East; greater than that of Ethan, Heman, Calcol, and Darda, who may have been classic Edomite sages (I Kings 4:31 f.). Solomon reputedly exchanged riddles and proverbs with the Queen of Sheba as well as with Hiram (I Kings 10:1). No matter how legendary the account, it indicates the conviction that exchange was possible and had occurred. Names of places and people in Israel's wisdom tradition are frequently foreign. Job was from Uz, most probably a part of Edom (1:1; cf. Gen. 31:2). The characters of the story seem to have been placed in localities famed for wisdom. Éliphaz was from Teman in Edom; Bildad from Shuah, in Assyria; and Zophar from Naamah, in Edom or Philistia (Job 2:11). Gressmann identifies Balaam, who must be related to Israel's wisdom tradition, with Bela, the first king of Edom, and thinks that Job may have been his successor.[19] Éduard Meyer thinks that Loqman, the prototype of the Greek Aesop, may have been of Edomite origin.[20] The proverbs of Agur and Lemuel are attributed to men with foreign names. In Ezek. 28:2–5 the tirade against Tyre recognized that city's reputation for human wisdom, which, in the city's own estimation, exceeded that of the legendary Danel. Isaiah, chapter 19, deprecates Egypt's trust in wisdom, a prophetic attitude that sometimes applied to Israel as well (Jer. 8:8). The chapter reveals the writer's intimate acquaintance with life in

[19] *Op. cit.*, p. 20.

[20] *Die Israeliten und ihre Nachbarstämme* (Halle: S. M. Niemeyer, 1906), p. 378.

Egypt, its industries, its dependence upon the Nile, and the sages acting as counselors in the court circles. Jeremiah recognizes that the wise in Babylon occupy a similar place (50:35; 51:47). Hezekiah's scribe, Shebnah, had a foreign name and may have been a foreigner. In a later era the writer of apocryphal Baruch stressed the superiority of Jewish wisdom over that of other peoples: "None of these have remembered the way of wisdom or known her paths" (2:23). What he means is that these other peoples had not equated their wisdom with the Jewish Law, as the people of Israel had come to do. The development of this Jewish bias against foreign wisdom we shall discuss in a later chapter. Jesus ben Sira was one of its promoters. But the very existence of the bias in a later era of greater religious control and exclusiveness indicates the presence of internationally current materials and ideas in Israel's culture.

The role of the sages and the public estimate of them were very similar in all lands. They were the schoolmasters and the court counselors, and in Israel they are sometimes equated with the scribes (Jer. 8:8 f.; Ben Sira 38:24—39:11). They held responsible positions: Amen-em-ope was controller of lands; Elishama, of Israel, was in charge of the archives (Jer. 36:20 f.). Their position was enviable. In the Instruction of Duauf we learn that "the scribe, every position at court is open to him." This position of privilege tended to make the sages exclusive and caste-conscious; they were often disdainful of others and satirized all other vocations, as Papyrus Lansing well demonstrates. The opening paragraph of the Instruction of Ptahhotep offers a notable exception to this trait; for it declares that the sage may learn something from all men, even from the slave girls at the mill. Gemser feels that wisdom was more democratic in Israel than in Egypt. He insists that the proverbial collections, unlike those of Egypt, were not directed at a single class, but at all.[21] Yet it seems that the nature of the material presented by the Hebrew sages must also have limited its influence to an educated class. The wise were men of leisure; they prided themselves on having traveled (Eccles. 4:15 f.; 10:7, 16 f.; Ben Sira 34:12 f.; 51:13). As teachers, they inculcated a respect for age, tradition, and authority— they were a conservative element in society.

The general similarities in literary form and subject matter of the Wisdom Literatures of the ancient Near East are obvious from even a casual comparison of the documents. Not infrequently there are illustrations, proverbs, metaphors, and stories that are shared. An exhaustive list of such specific items held in common would be quite impressive but would hardly serve our purpose here. Two or three will suffice as illustrations. For example, the story of the clever sentence of Solomon is reported to have been identified in twenty-two versions among various peoples of the ancient East. It is Gressmann's opinion that the story originated in India.[22] In Ben Sira 18:9 we are told that "the number of a man's days at the most are a hundred years." This seems difficult to understand in the light of the psalmist's expectation of seventy or eighty. But in Papyrus Insinger we are told that "even though the life of man reaches a hundred years, a fourth of it is lost" (17:21). As a final illustration we may cite the fourth chapter of the Teaching of Amen-em-ope, which draws a contrast between the passionate and the tranquil man by comparing the fate of the

[21] Op. cit., p. 6; cf. Prov. 3:8 f.   [22] Op. cit., p. 11.

tree in the forest, which is cut down for kindling, with that of the tree in the garden, which is carefully tended by its owner. Both in the First Psalm and in Jer. 17:5–8, the figure of the tree is used to describe the good or "tranquil" man for the Hebrews, though the evil man is described as chaff. The metaphor of the flourishing tree is hinted at in many places in the Old Testament.

The task of the wisdom movement of each nation—Babylon, Egypt, and Israel—is to possess wisdom, an understanding of the highest ends of life and of the means of attaining them. This task involved a natural human search and discovery through the use of human reason and an empirical analysis of experience. In each country, however, the wisdom movement also seems to point to a concurrent conviction that wisdom was a divine possession and that it was ultimately the gift of the gods to men, whether by man's use of the reason he possessed as creature or by supernatural powers and special gifts beyond the natural faculties and lying outside the compass of empirical verification. The relative emphasis placed upon the natural and supernatural ways of attaining wisdom in the main documents of Israel's wisdom movement will be dealt with in a later chapter. Here we note very briefly that the same double emphasis existed in Babylon and Egypt.

In Babylon the priest at the shrine was called the "knowing one" (*mudu*) or the "wise one" (*ummann*). The first line of the fragmentary Poem of the Righteous Sufferer reads: "I will praise the Lord of Wisdom." It was probably addressed to Ea, god of knowledge. The Babylonian Book of Proverbs assumes that wisdom is accessible to all. But Stephen Langdon, in a quotation from Ebeling's text, gives us a clue which indicates that wisdom might also be considered as the special divine gift granted only to select persons: "The functions of using the reed as many as the god Ea has created, the rituals of the holy curse, the acts of the atonement by omens of heaven on earth, as many as these be, the totality of the sum of wisdom, the mystery of the incantation priest—to comprehend all these things."[23] We recall that in Israel wisdom came by dreams and by a special gift of spirit, later often interpreted as wisdom, enabling men to do unusual things as leaders and in interpretation of the divine will (Gen. 37:7 ff.; Exod. 35:30 ff.; II Kings 2:9; Neh. 9:20.).

In Egypt we also find wisdom and the wise associated with magic, divine secrets, and priesthood, though proverbial writers in Egypt, perhaps more than elsewhere, scorn magic and cult rites. In the Admonitions of a Prophet we are given a picture of the destruction of the city, which seems to hint at the danger of having cult secrets become common property:

Nay, but the splendid judgment hall; its writings are taken away; the secret place is laid bare—
Nay, but the magic spells are divulged . . . . for the people have them in mind.
Nay, but the scribes of the sack, their writings are destroyed.[24]

That which had been the prerogative of a few had been usurped by all; apparently, the "scribes," who may be identified with the wise, were the possessors of the secrets. In Papyrus Lansing the pupil, Wen-endy-Amon, eulogizes his instructor, Neb-Maat-Re-Nakht, and seems to indicate that

[23] Op. cit., p. 6.   [24] Erman, op. cit., p. 99.

he was a priest as well as a scribe: "Thou art beauteous of hands when bearing the censer in front of the lord of gods at every procession of his" (13:5). Similarly, in the Teaching of Amen-em-ope, the pupil or son, Harmakher, performs the roles of a priest (2:15—3:7). One of the reasons for the ascription of wisdom to Solomon and to other oriental monarchs may be due to the fact that they were all considered to be possessors of special divine powers because of their position as anointed rulers. Solomon's wisdom as a judge made people fear him, for they saw that "the wisdom of God was in him" (I Kings 3:28). Leaders like Moses and Joshua and their aids possessed the "spirit of wisdom" (Deut. 34:9; 1:13; Num. 11:16 ff.). Humbert feels that the ascription of Ecclesiastes to Solomon is an adoption of the pattern followed in Egypt, where the wise also attributed their words to rulers.[25]

We have seen that the political and commercial relationships of Israel with Egypt and Mesopotamia led to intimate literary relatedness, as exemplified in the wisdom materials of the three lands. The writers of the Old Testament acknowledge this relation; usually they are proud of it. We also have evidence that the status and role of the sages in the three lands were similar and that some of their specific materials formed a common stock. Now we have noted that, for all, wisdom is somehow rooted in the divine (for Israel this point will be elaborated later). Finally, the wisdom materials seem to show that, despite great differences in religion and cult, all the nations involved may be said to have had a single basic culture.

[25] Paul Humbert, *Recherches sur les sources égyptiennes de la littérature sapientiale d'Israel* (Neuchâtel: Secrétariat de l'Université, 1929), p. 5.

Since our concern is only with the Hebrew wisdom materials, this common view of life demands no full exposition here. It is only hinted at to suggest the context of the Hebrew wisdom movement. The core of the general cultural viewpoint held in common rests on the conviction that existence is fundamentally rational and moral. The divine rule, to whatever deity assigned, is held to be constant and intelligent. The divine order rewards those who discover and obey it; it punishes those who transgress it—life is morally interpreted. The Wisdom Literatures of the three peoples show concretely how goodness was very much the same for all, whether they acknowledged Re, Marduk, or Yahweh. The "good citizen" of any of the three would be like the one from either of the other two, since restraint, honesty, kindness, industry, domestic virtue, respect for age, a sense of civic duty, piety, humility, and mercy were virtues extolled by all the wisdom teachers. Belief in a moral rule is a presupposition of the sages of all three lands, who proceed on the assumption that it is discoverable by, or given to, men. When they despair of this, as the reflective essays among the wisdom materials of each country often tend to do, they fall into a pessimism which makes life lose its meaning. But when faith in the discovery or revelation of wisdom stood high, there was confidence that goodness would be rewarded.

It may be noted that this reward for goodness was usually promised for this world by the sages. This was also true in Egypt, despite the convictions about future rewards that prevailed there. In Amen-em-ope the instructor promises his pupil: "Thou wilt find my words a storehouse of life, and thy body will prosper upon earth" (4:1 f.). The same

faith in reward on earth is the support of the admonition
to follow "tranquillity" (7:7–10):

> As to all the tranquil in the temple,
> they say, "Great is the good pleasure of Re."
> Hold fast to the tranquil man, (thus) wilt thou find life,
> (and) thy body shall prosper on earth.

A corollary of this faith is a doctrine of duty. In the Babylonian Book of Proverbs this expectation of rewards on
earth is also present:

> Give food to eat and wine to drink.
> Seek justice, feed and honour parents.
> In such an one will God have pleasure;
> It is pleasing unto Shamash who will reward him with
> good.[26]

The Hebrews had a similar doctrine with which we shall
deal later in detail.

A second element in the Wisdom Literatures of Egypt,
Babylon, and Israel showing a common cultural viewpoint
is the keen awareness, expressed in all, that in this morally
and rationally governed world man is a creature. He is
finite, ignorant, and subject to moral failure. "Man know-
eth not how the morrow will be," says Amen-em-ope; "the
events of the morrow are in the hands of God" (19:13). And
in 24:12 f. of the same document we are told: "Verily man
is clay and straw, God is his fashioner." For the English
proverb, "Man proposes, but God disposes," we have an
Egyptian antecedent which says: "The words which man
say are one thing, the things which god doeth are another."
The idea that there is a divine design and providence, at

[26] Langdon, *op. cit.*, p. 90.

least partially hidden, is not uniquely Hebrew. The Babylonian Poem of the Righteous Sufferer speaks in the same
mood for the Mesopotamian tradition:

> What seems good to one's self is worthlessness before God.
> What to his mind is despicable is good before God
> Who compares the will of the gods in the midst of the heavens?
> The counsel of God is full of knowledge, who understands it?
> Where have beclouded humanity comprehended the way of God?
> He who was alive yesterday evening is dead today.[27]

The Hebrew commentary on such a passage is naturally
"For my ways are not your ways, saith the Lord" (Isa.
55:8 f.).

Overconcern with this awareness of finitude and with
man's apparent inability to discover or receive the truth
about life was frequently brought on by individual or national calamity. It resulted in a loss of moral direction and
drive and produced a deep pessimism, which led either to
tragic despair or to a languid eudaemonism. The Egyptian
Admonitions of a Prophet, the Babylonian Dialogue of
Pessimism, and the Hebrew Job illustrate the tragic despair
tendency; and Ecclesiastes, the Dialogue with His Soul of
One Who Is Tired of Life, and the Admonitions of a
Prophet portray the eudaemonistic.

But these moods of utter despair and attendant moral
irresponsibility never become normative. The belief in justice and its vindication abides; the denial of a rational and
moral governance of all life remains the exception. In Egypt
the world beyond will make all things right. The Dialogue
with His Soul of One Who Is Tired of Life expresses the

[27] *Ibid.*, p. 41.

faith that Toth, the scribe and judge, would defend him. The Babylonian Tabi-utul-Enlil, who never asks for death, continues to believe that his tears will cease and that a day of grace will dawn, though he may not have a true rationale for such a faith.[28] Neither does Job become entirely hopeless; for he believes that God is the creator and ruler of all and that he rules in moral justice. This moral rule will be vindicated despite the fact that Job may not learn its way. This is not the place for discussing the ways out of despair presented by the Hebrew wisdom movement. Our concern here is simply to indicate that this movement followed in the wake of, and stood in intimate relation to, wisdom traditions of Egypt and Babylon, which were governed by a view of life basically like the Hebrew.

It has become increasingly clear that Hebrew wisdom fits into its context. The role of the sages and their methods are similar; their lessons have the same practical ends. The literary forms produced and materials used correspond; and all are concerned with divine justice based on a cosmic moral order. That was to be expected among peoples whose political and commercial intercourse had been very close over a period of centuries.

[28] *Ibid.*, pp. 67 ff.

CHAPTER II

THE NATIONALIZATION OF WISDOM

WISDOM included a knowledge of the mysteries of the
gods, as well as an understanding of the practical
conduct that would bring a man prosperity and happiness
in life; and some in every nation of the ancient East were
engaged in the search for wisdom. As we have seen, the
social position, the methods of work, the problems dealt
with, and the purposes of all wisdom seekers were very
similar, regardless of nationality. The extant Wisdom Literature of Egypt, Mesopotamia, and Palestine makes this
clear. The wisdom seekers of the Hebrews arose much later
than those of the Nile and the Euphrates and depended
upon the earlier seekers in many ways. But, despite this
foreign tutelage, the entire Hebrew wisdom movement ultimately comes under the hegemony of the Hebrew national
and religious tradition. Today its records are an integral
part of the Jewish religious heritage; and the wisdom seekers ended up by becoming teachers of the Hebrew Law. We
must here note the steps by which and the manner in which
this transition and this assimilation were accomplished.

The capacity of Hebrew religion to assimilate foreign
forms and ideas is historically attested in many ways. Students of Hebrew civilization and culture have repeatedly
shown how specific feats and rites, once celebrated in honor
of other deities, particularly the fertility gods of Canaan,
were ultimately incorporated in the Yahweh cultus. They

have shown that Hebrew religious architecture was almost wholly borrowed. In the phenomena of religion, Yahweh and his people were indebted to many sources. The great diversity and the wide extent of the materials and concepts taken over and the thorough assimilation that took place attest the vitality and high integrity of the Hebrew religious consciousness as expressed in the cult of Yahweh. Thus the rules of life and the ideas of human existence, which were the wisdom given to men by such Babylonian and Egyptian deities as Ea, Shamash, Re, Toth, and Horus, were attributed to Yahweh; and Yahweh became the guarantor of the rewards that resulted from obeying the rules. Finally, it falls out that only a Jew who knows and obeys the Mosaic Law is capable of possessing or profiting by this wisdom.

In the canonical Wisdom Literature the process of nationalizing the Hebrew wisdom movement has hardly begun. Its writers give no evidence of being zealous patriots; for their writings contain few allusions and no explicit references to the long history of the Hebrew people, to which the prophetic, historical, and devotional writers went so constantly for illustrative material. In all the canonical wisdom material, there is only the single reference to Solomon, son of David, who ruled at Jerusalem (Eccles. 1:1, 13 f.). No other personalities or incidents of the national story are mentioned in Proverbs, Job, or Ecclesiastes. In Job, it is true, we are told that God, who watches over nations as well as over individuals, sets up a godless king over a stubborn people (34:29 f.). This may apply to Israel; but it must be remembered that wisdom writers in every land believed that the god set up kings over his nation; and, at least in Israel, the wise thought that God was universal and appointed kings and presided over the destinies of all nations (Prov. 8:15). The general character of the reference is here also indicated by the use of the word בּוּר.

The canonical wisdom writers also ignore particularistic national religious concepts. National election, the day of Yahweh, the Covenant and the Law, the Messiah, the priesthood and the cultus, prophets and prophecy—all these are basic motivations in Hebrew religious thinking; but the early wisdom writers make little or no use of them. This is all the more striking if we remember that most of this literature was probably produced after the Exile and that the latest document, Ecclesiastes, is commonly dated about 200 B.C.[1] This was an era when the Jews were especially exclusive and conscious of their peculiar religious institutions.

In explanation of this neglect of the national religious heritage it may be urged that these writers were addressing all thoughtful people, regardless of nation or cult; or, as in the case of Job, that they were putting their ideas into the mouths of non-Israelite characters. Even so, it is still remarkable that they never commend their religion to these foreigners. Later wisdom writers, such as Ben Sira and the men who wrote IV Maccabees, Wisdom of Solomon, and the Letter of Aristeas, are all eager to appeal to non-Jews. Just because of this they eulogize their national history and their national religious institutions. This striking neglect of Jewish history and religion by the canonical wisdom writers clearly indicates that the Hebrew wisdom movement had not yet been integrated into the national religion.

[1] R. H. Pfeiffer, *Introduction to the Old Testament* (New York: Harper & Bros., 1941), p. 731.

A study of the divine names used in the early Wisdom Literature is similarly revealing. The oldest strata of the Book of Proverbs use "Yahweh," the proper Hebrew name for deity, almost exclusively.[2] The little section (30:1-9), known as the Words of Agur, uses "Yahweh," "Eloah," "Elohim," "Kᵉdoshim," and "El," the last being used twice. In this section an apparent quotation of Ps. 18:31 changes "Yahweh" to "Eloah." The first nine chapters of the Book of Proverbs, probably the youngest in the document, also use "Yahweh," though other terms occur more frequently than elsewhere (2:5, 17; 3:4; 9:10).

It is the opinion of Johannes Fichtner that this frequent use of the proper name for deity in the oldest strata occurs entirely without reflection. The writers are quite unconscious of its particularistic meaning; for them it simply means "deity" in a general sense. He also thinks that he detects in the occasional use of more general terms in the later sections, and particularly in the change of the name for deity in the passage quoted from Psalm 18, a conscious avoidance of the personal name.[3] It seems that there is hardly sufficient evidence to warrant the latter part of his statement. But the former part of it seems justified, especially since the Book of Proverbs, in its oldest strata, fails to make any use whatever of the peculiar relation which Yahweh bears to an Israelite. He is not described as the God of my "fathers" or of "our fathers," nor is he "our God" or "your God"—uses of the

---

[2] Proverbs, chaps. 25-27, once; 28-29, five times; 10-15, twenty times; 16:1—22:16, thirty-seven times; 22:17—24:22, five times; 31:10-31, once. In all these sections the general term "Elohim" occurs only once, in Prov. 25:2.

[3] *Die altorientalische Weisheit in ihr israelitisch-jüdische Ausprägung: Eine Studie zur Nationalisierung der Weisheit in Israel* (Giessen: A. Töpelmann, 1933), p. 98.

possessive which are very common in the Old Testament
books outside the wisdom documents.[4]
The dialogue of Job, including the speech of Elihu, uses
the proper name "Yahweh" only once (12:9). And this is
commonly counted as a *lapsus calami* for אֱלוֹהַ, for which
there is manuscript evidence. This book seems to delight in
using such archaic and universally accepted terms for
"deity" as "El," "Elóah," and "Shaddai." In his universalistic thinking the writer seems to avoid the personal
name of Israel's God. Apparently, it has not occurred to
him to identify this national deity with the universal divine
he contemplates. Fichtner sees in this rejection of the term
"Yahweh" "ein Ausdruck für dem Tatbestand dass jeg-
liche völkisch begrenzte Gottes benennung dem universa-
listischen Glauben und Denken der Weisen des Dialogs nicht
angemessen war."[5] This would indicate that for the sage the
word "Yahweh" was still too strongly colored by tribal
and national hues to permit its safe use in discussions which
had a universal interest.
The Book of Ecclesiastes also completely omits the use of
the name "Yahweh." We shall see that it was precisely this
identification of Yahweh with the universal God-concept,
not consciously present in the canonical Wisdom Literature,
that characterized the later Jewish wisdom materials. And
the identification had a double effect: it furthered the uni-
versalization of the Jewish religious outlook, and it made
the Hebrew wisdom movement consciously and integrally
a part of the Jewish religious tradition.

[4] There are two exceptions, not in the oldest strata: Proverbs 30:9 uses "my God"; and Proverbs 2:7 uses "her God."

[5] *Op. cit.*, pp. 98 f.

While the canonical wisdom writers make no conscious use of the national religious tradition, there are signs that they were touched by its spirit and shared in its practices or, at least, were aware of them. One is somehow reminded of a contemporary secular novelist or essayist who uses metaphors that betray a cultural acquaintance with Christianity. For example, the influence of the prophets seems evident. When the Book of Proverbs (21:27) tells us that the sacrifice of the wicked is an abomination that cannot atone for crime, it makes us think of Amos and Isaiah. In a later stratum of the same book (3:9 f.), Yahweh's blessing is dependent upon a faithful performance of the sacrifices: "Honour the Lord with your substance, with the first fruits of all your produce, so will your barns be filled with grain and your vats will be filled with wine." This is a close parallel to the doctrine of rewards in the Book of the Prophet Malachi (3:9 f.). As the author of victory, God is contrasted with the horse, a favorite prophetic comparison as well.

Sometimes the Book of Proverbs has a Deuteronomic flavor. The instruction of parents must be fastened on the mind and hung about the neck so that, sleeping or waking, walking or sitting, the son may be reminded of it (6:20–22; 7:3). In a similar manner Deuteronomy hopes to make the Law a constant guide and protection (6:4–9). Another Deuteronomic touch is provided by the assurance that "the upright" will possess the land as an inheritance (2:21; 10:30; cf. also 4:21, 38; 15:4; 19:10; 21:23; 24:4; 25:19; 26:1). For the sage, too, this probably referred to Israel's land. While the admonitions and promises here cited can be paralleled from Egyptian sources, the language is typically Deuteronomic.

Proverbs also tells us that God protects the way of his "pious ones," using a term incessantly employed in Hebrew devotional literature, especially in the Psalter (2:8; cf. Pss. 16:3; 30:4; 31:23; 34:9; 37:28; 50:5; 85:8; 97:10).

That the Book of Proverbs explicitly refers to the Mosaic Law is doubtful. In the Words of Agur we are told that "every word of God is tested." This is a difficult passage to interpret. Fichtner maintains that this refers to the words spoken by the sages. If this be true, it is the first instance we have in which their instruction is declared to be God's word. Toy, however, insists that the statement refers to the Mosaic Code. If this be true, we have here an allusion to the national religious heritage and the earliest approximation of wisdom to the Law. Toy's view claims as its support the fact that the verse containing this sentence is a quotation of Ps. 18:30. That psalm does refer to the Mosaic Code.[6] It is naturally very difficult to decide just when the quotation from Psalms was inserted in the Book of Proverbs. The wisdom movement was characteristically independent in its ethical teaching. Thus Proverbs is both more emphatic and more specific than the Mosaic Law on the subject of the care of one's enemies (Prov. 24:17, 29; 25:21; cf. also Lev. 19:18). This warns us to be cautious about finding any reference to the Law in the wisdom section ascribed to Agur.

Like the Book of Proverbs, Job contains vague reflections of Hebrew religious institutions and language. God is the dispenser of rain and snow; he has stretched out the heavens and treads upon the billows. Sheol lies open before him.

[6] Prov. 30:5; Crawford H. Toy, *The Book of Proverbs: A Critical and Exegetical Commentary* (New York: Charles Scribner's Sons, 1908), pp. 522 f.; and Fichtner, *op. cit.*, pp. 87 f.

God's reproof and instruction are a sign of his favor and a blessing to the man who receives them (5:10, 17; 9:8; 26:6). Under cultic oath Job swears that he is innocent of a list of sins that are typically Jewish: He has not committed adultery, mistreated his slaves, or neglected the poor and the orphan; he has not put his trust in riches; he has never even thought of worshiping the heavenly bodies; he has not gloated over the downfall of his enemies; and he has kept the laws of hospitality (31:26-28; probably a spurious section). Job's complaint that his way is hedged in by God occurs in a metaphor that is found elsewhere only in the Book of Lamentations (3:7).

The Book of Ecclesiastes is separate from the national Jewish religious outlook not merely in the sense that, like Proverbs and Job, its writer fails to make explicit references to its institutions but also because he seems specifically to deny the active and purposive character of God, which is a basic quality in the Hebrew religious outlook. Upon this outlook rested all of Hebrew culture, not merely its peculiar religious forms and institutions. In contrast, Koheleth's God is not Providence, but blind fate. If there is any purpose in God's way, man cannot know it. He lives in a world of opposites in which all events take place according to their proper time cycle and with no moral reference. It is noteworthy that Koheleth rests his case for the uselessness of life upon the Genesis stories of Creation and the Fall. Man, created like the animals, dies like them. He is taken from dust and returns to dust (Eccles. 3:18-20; cf. also Gen. 2:7, 19; 3:19). Man lives under the curse of toil, illness, and struggle pronounced against him in the Garden (5:14-16). He refutes the optimistic Hebrew view of life by examining the very mythology on which it builds. Probably because of too much Hellenistic influence, he is culturally a stranger among his own people. Religious institutions and the national tradition of election are ignored.

The canonical Wisdom Literature makes scarcely any reference to the mercy of God. Proverbs mentions it but once (28:13). Job expresses the view that God might be forgiving and overlook some guilt (7:21; 11:6). But it is clear that as a divine attribute the concept of mercy is entirely secondary and quite insignificant. God's righteousness and justice are the basis upon which his relations with men are conceived; the faith of Proverbs is built upon them, and Job and Ecclesiastes question and deny them.

This striking omission of the concept of mercy is another bit of evidence that the canonical wisdom material presents an outlook that is not integrated with the national religious tradition. In Israel's religion, mercy plays as great a role as righteousness and justice; here it is lacking, because it was a quality shown particularly to Israel, who could count on God's mercy because they were an elect people. This mercy, historically shown in their deliverance from Egypt *before* the sealing of the national covenant at Sinai, was the seal of the national election. It was an act of initial grace on the part of God, which, for Israel, permanently endowed the character of God with the quality of mercy. And this mercy, in the last analysis, always transcended the legal covenant. The hope for rebuilding and return, which inspires the prophets and literally keeps Hebrew faith alive, is founded upon this divine attribute. By virtually ignoring it the canonical wisdom writers remain outside the national religious orbit. Moreover, by the same token, they also assert that independence of spirit and self-reliance which has often made modern interpreters refer to them as "humanists." To this we shall return.

When we leave the canonical documents and turn to the later wisdom writings of the Jews, we find that the movement that produced them was rapidly becoming an integral part of the national religious tradition. The later writings eulogize Hebrew history and the religious institutions of Israel, and their conviction that wisdom is attainable depends more and more upon the resources of Jewish religious faith. In the Book of Wisdom of Jesus ben Sira, probably produced in Jerusalem about 200 B.C., we can actually see this transition taking place. The book is a bit later than Ecclesiastes, whose author Ben Sira may have known.

Ben Sira's grandson came to Alexandria in the thirty-eighth year of the reign of Euergetes II (132 B.C.). Soon thereafter he translated his grandfather's book into Greek. He provided the translation with a prologue of his own, in which he displays a missionary enthusiasm which is interested in reaching both the Gentiles and the Jews living in Alexandria. He hopes his work may "profit them that are without"; but he is also very much concerned about the Jews who, though "lovers of learning," apparently no longer know the Hebrew tongue. Therefore he has prepared a translation, that he might make available, "in the land of their sojourning," this book for those who are "already disposed, in regard to their ethical culture, to live according to the Law." These "sojourners" may, and very probably do, include Greeks as well as Jews.

The grandson of Jesus ben Sira insists that Israel deserves a great reputation for wisdom because it has been given so many things in the Law and the prophets. Thus he both exalts the entire national and religious tradition of Judaism and makes wisdom dependent upon, and a product of, that tradition. As a sage he is empirical and scientific; he looks for truth everywhere. But as a religious man he has found in the Mosaic Law, properly understood, the highest expression of the moral values generated by the Hebrew wisdom movement. His object is to safeguard the Law and its values. He has recently come from sheltered Palestine, and he fears that the Law's relation to knowledge may not be understood by the Jews in the syncretistic setting of Alexandria. What better can he do than translate his grandfather's work on wisdom, in which the results of scientific and philosophic inquiry are rooted in the religion of the Law?

Psychologically, the reaction of Ben Sira's grandson to the scene in Alexandria is quite a normal one. He is probably frightened by the great stimulation which Greek culture has given Jewish minds. His prologue seems to imply that he is troubled by the free speculation of the Diaspora Jews. He does not wish the Law to lose its central position in their life and thought; for he loves the rigid Palestinian tradition. Recently many of his fellows had died as martyrs for it; so he toils to provide in Greek a book in which wisdom is companioned and defined by the Law. He hopes that this will help the Alexandrians to root their speculations in the Jewish religious tradition.[7]

The translator of Ben Sira felt that the national tradition was passing through an acute crisis. This was true. Cheyne indorses Mommsen's view that the foundation of Alexan-

[7] Andreas Eberharter, *Das Buch Jesus Sirach, oder Ecclesiasticus* (Bonn: Peter Hanstein, 1925), p. 9.

dria was as serious and critical an event for the Jews as the conquest of Jerusalem and the Exile to Babylon. Many Jews were much more frightened than elated; for never before had paganism been so attractive as in this center of the Diaspora in Egypt. The reaction of Ben Sira's grandson was decidedly progressive; he seeks to make the Jewish religious tradition available to the Diaspora in the Greek tongue. However, in strictly conservative circles the translation of the Hebrew Bible into Greek was greatly deplored, much as translation of the Koran is deplored by orthodox Moslems today. Tradition says that a fast was proclaimed on the day the Septuagint appeared and that the translation was compared to the golden calf in heinousness.[8]

Fear for the continued integrity of the religious tradition was increased by the repeated apostasy of large sections of the people, even in the homeland. This was clearly illustrated by the national division at the time of the outrages of Antiochus Epiphanes in 165 B.C. (I Macc. 1:11–15). Ben Sira eulogizes Simeon, the son of Jochanan, as a strict observer of the Law (50:1 ff.). But Josephus tells us that the famous priest's relatives and descendants were victims of the Hellenizing tendency. His cousin was a tax farmer in Palestine, whose immoralities sapped the foundations of Jewish life. His sons, Jason and Menelaus, were traitors, who promoted the paganizing movement.

When Jesus ben Sira wrote his book at the opening of the second century, this struggle for the survival of the faith of Israel in its integrity was already on and was constantly becoming more intense. It created a demand for the more complete consolidation of the cultural and spiritual resources of the nation, especially in the circles most open to apostasy, the cultured circles in which the wisdom movement thrived. And it had to be presented in such a form as to be palatable to the enlightened folk who belonged to this group. The strategy was to make the Law the core of the entire national religious heritage, and Ben Sira made his contribution by bringing the hitherto almost completely independent wisdom movement under the domain of the Law. In this sense his book, as well as his grandson's translation of it, was a tract for the times. Ewald has called it a *Zwischenschrift*, a piece of literature marking the transition of the wisdom movement from its earlier independence to its ultimate assimilation by the rabbinic legal movement. The sages become able and persuasive apologists and interpreters of the Jewish religious institutions, both to Greeks and to Hellenistically minded Jews. In this new role Jesus ben Sira leads the way.

Ben Sira does not wholly rule out free inquiry and the empirical method in the discovery of wisdom. In his book, wisdom is not yet wholly defined by the Law, nor is the search for it limited simply to a study of the Law. As in the earlier Book of Proverbs, there are admonitions to seek wisdom that omit all reference to the Law. For example, to become wise one must seek the companionship of the wise and study the rich store of proverbs which is the accumulated heritage of the wisdom movement (1:25; 6:34; 8:8; 9:14). One must be an attentive pupil, eager to learn (3:29; 6:35). The wise give oral instruction, not specifically delimited by a written document (4:24; 6:33).

On the other hand, with Ben Sira the Law does become the touchstone by which to measure the results of the search for wisdom. The book makes "the fear of the Lord" synonymous with the keeping of the Mosaic Code (2:16; 23:27; 32:15 f.), which is a cue permitting us to equate wisdom with the Law in those places in which it is equated with "the fear of the Lord" (1:14, 16, 18, 20, 27; 15:1; 19:20; 21:11; 40:27). If in these places one may read the word "Law" instead of the words "fear of the Lord," the Law is a source of wisdom. The Law, then, is the sum of wisdom, and wisdom is the consummation of the Law. In many other places Law and wisdom are brought together; meditation in the Law and the mastery of it are the avenues that lead to wisdom (1:26; 6:37; 9:14 f.; 15:1; 19:17; 24:22 f.; 33:2; 34:8; 39:1 ff.). A man who fears God is preferable to a clever man who disobeys the Law (19:24).

In discussing the connection between the phrase "the fear of the Lord" and wisdom, dealt with above, J. A. F. Gregg maintains that in the Wisdom of Solomon "the fear of the Lord" does not equal wisdom but alludes to its inscrutability. For Ben Sira and for those who followed him, the Law, being a divine gift, was always in a measure inscrutable; and wisdom, which was equated with it, consisted especially in recognizing this.[9] The surrender of the Jewish wisdom movement to the Law, beginning with Ben Sira, results ultimately, as we shall see later, in a shift from reliance upon human reason to a dependence upon divine grace and transcendent faith.

We must emphasize that with Ben Sira the Hebrew wisdom movement has taken firm rootage in the particularistic

[9] *The Wisdom of Solomon* (Cambridge: At the University Press, 1912), p. xxii.

Jewish religious tradition. It had begun as a secular movement which could make no use of the too tribalistic religious heritage and relied wholly on man's natural gifts. As time went on, especially in the era recorded by Proverbs, chapters 1–9, the leaders of the movement discovered that religion and its foundations are valid and important in a rational, critical outlook upon the world, and they began to find the deep bases of reason and ethics. Gradually the wise men were converted to the national religious tradition, which did have a moral interpretation of life that enshrined these bases. Yet their conversion was not to some of the narrow dogmatisms from which they had stood aside in the beginning. Jewish religious thinking had also advanced, as II Isaiah bears ample witness. By their return to religion the sages helped to lift all of it to an entirely new level, universalistic in outlook. Their discoveries in the natural realm and in the histories and cultures of all peoples were poured into the national religious tradition and assimilated by it. A comparison of the pre-Exilic writers with documents like the Wisdom of Solomon and IV Maccabees would illustrate the difference which the new alliance of the wisdom movement and religion produced in the latter. It is only a part of the truth to say that wisdom was nationalized; it is equally necessary to say that Jewish religion (theology) was universalized. The recognition by the wise, in Proverbs, chapters 1–9, that the "fear" of the Lord is "wisdom"—namely, their return to religion—helped to make this possible.

From now on, wisdom, as a human possession, comes by diligent study of the Law of Moses. Fichtner seems justified in his conclusion that, beginning with Ben Sira, the Law

was explicitly normative for the Jewish sages.[10] The accumulated lore of human experience must all be brought under the Law's jurisdiction; and this single concrete code at last becomes the arbiter of all right action. Instead of being guided by this or that coterie of sages, where group differences and individual differences provided intellectual stimulus, there is now, for the wisdom movement, a single definitive embodiment of the divine will by which all who seek the way of righteousness and life are to be governed.

Ben Sira also exalts the national religious tradition by celebrating the cultus. He is a devotee of the Temple and its priests, who must be honored by bringing them all the sacrifices that are their due (7:29–31). There is a large section in his book in which he eulogizes the national heroes, which is in itself a new feature for a wisdom writer. But in this list of worthies it is notable that he gives an especially large place to Aaron, the founder of the national priesthood (45:6 ff.). His personal enthusiasm for, and delight in, Jewish ritual is clearly evident in his description of the magnificent appearance of the high priest, Simeon, and his entourage at the Temple services (50:1–24). He is fond of the incense mingled with the sacrifices and speaks of the holy lamp in the temple. He reminds his readers that even the phases of the moon were ordained by divine decree to mark out the festal days of the Jewish national religion (7:9; 24:15; 26:17; 33:8). Ben Sira is a much-traveled Jew and is proud of the fact; he has visited many nations and observed many customs and rites, but his heart is always in Jerusalem.

This wisdom writer of the transitional period is also con-

[10] *Op. cit.*, pp. 79 ff.

scious of a divine national election. Israel is unique among the nations; she is "the Lord's portion" (17:17–21). When the Divine Wisdom, God's eternal possession, was seeking for a place on earth where she might alight and make her home, God directed her to the temple in Jerusalem. So she ministered in the temple and dwelt among "the glorified people." (24:9–12). The last is a phrase popular with the apocalyptists.

The descent of the Divine Wisdom to teach men is also a theme in the latest section of the Book of Proverbs. There, however, it is discussed without any national reference; Wisdom does not enter a religious shrine but seeks men out in the streets and highways (Prov. 1:20 ff.; 8:1 ff.).

But, for this later sage, Israel was the Lord's first-born. God himself dwelt in Jerusalem, whence he ruled the world (36:11 ff.). God's Covenant binds him to Israel as to no other people; it is an everlasting relationship (17:12; 28:7). Ben Sira even seems to envisage the traditional final judgment by which God will usher in the triumph of Israel over its enemies. The wild winds, fire, hail, famine, scorpions, and vipers will play their role when the consummation comes that brings the wicked enemies of the nation to destruction (2:7–11; 16:11 f.; 17:29; 28:2–5; 51:8).

This consciousness of national election also helps to explain Ben Sira's emphasis upon the divine mercy. We have seen that this was absent in the canonical wisdom writers. For this writer God is as great in mercy as he is in righteousness; there is mercy for those who adhere to Yahweh and also for those who return to him. The initial act of mercy, the rescue from Egypt, on which the Covenant of national

election was founded, has deeply colored Ben Sira's idea of
God. But his appeal to the divine mercy arises also from an
awareness of human frailty not so evident in the Book of
Proverbs (18:5 ff.). This stress of human weakness inti-
mates a surrender of a measure of that freedom and independence claimed or sought by the canonical wisdom writers. It is the basis for the admission of a larger amount of
"grace" than they desired or permitted. Man's hope lay
ultimately not in his own reason and understanding but in
God's goodness. This turn in Ben Sira must be related to his
relative preference for the devout man of inferior understanding.

Like all other documents that display pride in the national heritage, the Wisdom of Jesus ben Sira makes much
use of the historical records of Israel. This is the first wisdom document that does so. To the writer the story of his
people appears as a record of the acts of divine providence.
The "famous men" are the great national heroes (chaps.
44–50). The stories of these men convince him that the Wisdom which all mankind seeks has its home in Israel. He re-
calls the signs and wonders by which his people were delivered from Egypt. The "generations of old" show that
trust in Yahweh is never misplaced (2:10; 36:6). The pride
that destroyed Sodom illustrates Yahweh's sovereignty
(16:18). Ben Sira also loves the land of Palestine and its natural scenes. The cedars of Lebanon, the cypresses of Her-
mon, the palm trees in the Jordan Valley, and the roses of
Jericho all fill his thought like the "amber waves of grain"
of a patriotic American (24:12–14).

It becomes quite clear that with Jesus ben Sira the wisdom

schools of Palestine had become Jewish schools. Wisdom is
no longer the common possession of the nations of the ancient Orient; it is a divinely appointed Jewish possession
in which the world may share. Wisdom has become particularistic. Yet the fruits of its earlier freedom and universal-
ism are not lost but are imparted to the national religious
tradition. The sages were men who had traveled, who knew
the lore of many lands, and who had had firsthand contact
with many types of people of divergent cultures. With the
nationalization of the wisdom movement, these sages did
not merely become subservient to the Law and to Jewish religious practice and thought, for theirs was not a negative
attitude of resignation, but they became personally and
consciously responsible for the national religious tradition.
The reasons that prompted men like Ben Sira to write show
this clearly. With their peculiarly fortunate heritage and
their sense of responsibility, it was inevitable that they
should bring to the religious outlook of Israel wider horizons that issued in broader applications and a more universal outlook. So, while in process of nationalization, the
wisdom movement functioned as a leaven.

Ben Sira's idea of God nicely illustrates this leavening
process. For him Yahweh is no mere tribal deity but the
creator and ruler of the universe and of all peoples. In the
wisdom tradition he is the first one consciously to identify
Israel's personal deity with the universal divine ruler. In
the early parts of Proverbs the use of God's proper name was
casual. In chapters 1–9 Yahweh is indeed the universal and
the giver of wisdom, but his special relation to Israel is not
discussed. Job and Ecclesiastes fail to use the personal name.

But in Ben Sira it is used consciously and purposely to emphasize that the God who has elected Israel, given it its Law and religious institutions, and presides over its historical destiny is the same as the universal creator and ruler. This equation is illustrated most graphically by 50:17 *b:* προσκυνῆσαι τῷ κυρίῳ παντοκράτορι θεῷ τῷ ὑπίστω. It uses both *kurios*, the term for the personal divine name, and *hupistos*, the term for the universal creator. Commenting on this passage, Fichtner says: "Danach ist Gott für Sir. deutlich Gott Israels und Schöpfer Gott in Einem."[11]

Like earlier wisdom writers, Ben Sira hymns the divine intelligence and power manifest in the material creation (1:9; 15:14; 16:24–30; 39:12–35; 42:15–43). But, unlike Job before him, he makes his nation's God the author of all this. In his creation of all and in his just governance, God is moved by the Divine Wisdom, which is built into and pervades his entire creation (1:9; 24:3–6). This is the same Wisdom which dwells in Jerusalem and ministers in the temple. There appears to be a complete harmony of material and moral sovereignty, since both are directly controlled by the same God.

The divine providence is cosmic. God's rule is exercised over nations through kings, whom he sets up and puts down to meet his moral demands (10:4, 8; 39:21 ff.). All men, irrespective of nation may and can fear God; the choice of life or death is offered to all (10:19–22; 15:17), and all peoples share in the divine mercy. As a shepherd leads his flock, so God trains and reproves all mankind (18:13).In so far as they fear the Lord, "the whole race of men" is

11 *Ibid.*, p. 100.

honorable. That "fear" is the glory of the "sojourner and stranger, foreigner and poor." But, as we have noted, this fear of the Lord is chiefly accomplished by an observance of the Mosaic Code. This Law is a national possession. But for Ben Sira it is also really a universally and eternally valid expression of truth, because it is the word of the only God, the Creator of all, and not merely one of the products of the Divine Wisdom of the universal God who is also Israel's Yahweh. The Law is actually the equal of this Divine Wisdom and lies beyond human comprehension; Divine Wisdom and the Law are co-extensive and coeternal. Describing this doctrine of Ben Sira, Wilhelm Schenke says: "Die göttliche, unergründlich tiefe, seit unvordenklichen Zeit existierenden, bei der Schöpfung wirksame Weisheit hat sich Gottes Befehl zufolge, in dem durch Moses vermittelten Gesetz von Sinai verkörpert."[12]

Ben Sira finds himself able to defend the national religious tradition by claiming divine authorship and indefinite and universal validity for its Law and for the institutions that flow from it. This is not the work of a little nation, he says in effect; this is the gift of the Creator and ruler of all the earth. In this Ben Sira and the wisdom writers who follow him are thoroughly "fundamentalistic." Accordingly, he declares that the Law is as reliable as the sacred lot (33:3). It is an eternal existence, a gift of God that is always valid.

[12] *Die Chokma (Sophia) in der jüdischen Hypostasenspekulation: Ein Beitrag zur Geschichte der religiösen Ideen im Zeitalter des Hellenismus* ("Skrifter Videnskapsselskapet," Vol. I [Kristiana, 1912]; "Historisk-filosofisk Klasse," No. 6 [Kristiana: A. W. Broggers, 1913]), p. 31.

It is more than a human instrument. Ben Sira feels that this should commend its acceptance by non-Jews, just as one type of contemporary missionary expects Christian doctrine to commend *itself* to Asiatics today. Neither Wisdom nor the Law is a Jewish product; both are divine gifts, God's word for all people.

Despite this strenuous effort of Ben Sira to make the Law universal, a sharply particularistic and nationalistic tendency remains. It may be coequal with the Divine Wisdom; and it may be the gracious gift of a universal God. Nevertheless, however cosmic its nature and divine its origin, it is a very concrete Jewish possession. Ben Sira really secured an "advantage" for the faithful Jew (36:1–10; cf. Rom. 3:1 ff.)! He hopes that foreigners may dramatically witness the power of Israel's God, so that they, like Israel, may know him as the universal ruler. By equating Divine Wisdom and the Law, these later sages helped greatly to lift the horizons of Israel's faith toward a universal outlook; but their efforts likewise illustrate how impossible it is to present as a religion for all peoples that which is the faith of one ethnic group. And by subjecting their movement to the Law, Ben Sira and those who followed had re-emphasized the position of the ethnic group in Israel's religious tradition.

Our analysis of the nationalization of the Jewish wisdom movement brings us to the document commonly known as the "Wisdom of Solomon." It probably appeared about seventy-five years after the Wisdom of Jesus ben Sira and is almost certainly the work of a Diaspora Jew in Alexandria. We may take the book as a testimony that the work of Ben

Sira's grandson had had the desired results; for, despite his familiarity with Hellenistic culture and ideas, the writer is very consciously and faithfully Jewish. He poses as King Solomon addressing the kings of the earth and urging them to be taught by wisdom (6:2). As in Ben Sira, rulers are appointed by God. The book is allusive rather than explicit; its historical references can be grasped only by those who are familiar with them. The writer wants to win proselytes (18:5).

The Wisdom of Solomon reveals some Hellenistic influence. The book employs technical Greek terms: the cosmos was made of formless matter (ὕλης αμόρφου), a Platonic idea (11:17). The four Stoic virtues are presented as the fruits of wisdom (8:7); and the attributes of wisdom include the terms λεπτόν and νοερόν, which originated as philosophical terms with Anaxagoras and the Stoics, respectively (7:22 f.). Most scholars feel that the writer had a Hellenistic belief in the pre-existence of the soul (8:19 f.). M. J. La Grange presents a penetrating reply to this view. He insists that the author simply adds the latter verse to cancel out an overemphasis upon the body in the former.[13] Like a good Jew, the writer is horrified at depicting the human form in painting and sculpture; yet his sense of artistic appreciation has developed sufficiently to enable him to recognize that the images he dreads and abhors can actually be beautiful (14:15, 17 ff.; 15:5; 14:19). This, too, is a new note in Jewish writers.

Despite these superficial accommodations to Hellenism,

---

[13] "Le Livre de la sagesse; sa doctrine des fins dernières," *Revue biblique*, IV (1907), 88 f.

the writer of the Wisdom of Solomon is stoutly Jewish. He is convinced that the national religious heritage is superior. Unlike Philo, he does not seek to equate it with that of the Greeks; he simply assumes that it is better. In this book, also, the universal God is Israel's Yahweh (9:1). Israel is an elect nation, a blood brotherhood bound by a divine covenant, sealed at Sinai (16:26; 18:13; 12:21; 18:9). He speaks of "our forefathers" made glorious by divine grace and by obedience (9:11; 18:22; 19:23). The last section of the book, beginning at chapter 10, is sometimes ascribed to a different author and consists of an idealized and allegorical interpretation of Israel's national history. Under the guidance of Wisdom and the Law the nation has obeyed God; therefore it will ultimately triumph and bring nations into subjection under it.

This book defines the Divine Wisdom in many ways. It is a spirit of God; a holy spirit; Creator of man, teacher, and guide. It dwells near God's throne, makes men friends of God, and gives them immortality (1:5, 7; 7:23–38; 8:1, 7, 13; 9:4, 17). Wisdom is a reflection of the everlasting light, a mirror of God's activity, and the likeness of his goodness (7:25 f.). It is one, and without destroying its identity, it enters into all that can receive it (7:27). Wisdom remains with God and does not become a demiurge or a soul for the world in any Platonic sense.

The writer also continues the identification of Wisdom and the Law that began with Ben Sira. He also speaks with reverence of the circumstances under which it was given to Israel (16:6; 18:4, 9).

In the Wisdom of Solomon the Law is likewise of universal validity. The writer condemns rulers for disobeying it (6:1–4); for they all hold their power, he maintains, under the universal ruler of nature and of man; and their responsibility is to Him. Fichtner feels that the reference here is not to the Jewish Law but to the universal divine law, the moral law of nature written in men's hearts. Oesterley, however, thinks that the passage refers to the Mosaic Code and consequently fails to see how it could address foreign kings.[14] Yet, being identified with Divine Wisdom as it is, there is really no longer any distinction between the Law of Moses and the moral law of nature in the hearts of all men (cf. Rom. 2:12–15, a New Testament application of this). Ideally, there is no longer any distinction between a universal and a Jewish Law, for the latter, too, is universally and eternally valid.

The Wisdom of Solomon does not fail to recognize that the Jew has an inestimable advantage in possessing this key to all existence as a special gift. For him alone does the universal law become concrete and articulate in the material Law. The writer both pities and blames the unfortunate pagans who must seek to understand the demands of a moral order without the benefit of this normative compass (13:1–9). God's sons, Israel, were the mediators by whom the world would receive the light of the Law (18:5). Like Divine Wisdom, the Law is the salvation of the world; but without the Law Wisdom cannot be understood—hence Israel's mission, for it alone knows the Law. There is, thus, an acute awareness of national election (3:9; 4:15; 12:7; 17:10). And, as in the Wisdom of Jesus ben Sira, there is an

---

[14] Fichtner, *Weisheit Salomos* (Tübingen: J. C. B. Mohr, 1938), pp. 25 f.; cf. also W. O. E. Oesterley, *The Wisdom of Solomon* (London: S.P.C.K., 1917), p. 40.

emphasis upon the divine mercy and a sense of dependence upon God growing out of the special gift he has made to his elect people.

In the Wisdom of Solomon, Wisdom also becomes synonymous with the Divine Word. Using a typically Semitic parallelism, this Alexandrine writer names both Wisdom and the Word as the divine instruments in creation (9:2). But there is a complementary, as well as synonymous, note. Wisdom alone is singled out to function in the creation of man. Intelligence seems to be the deepest thing in Wisdom. In the Word it is power. The Word heals. It is the real support of the believers; and, in the great events of the Exodus, it leaped from the divine throne to slay the first-born (16: 12, 26; 18:15 f.). It has apparently reached that degree of personification and hypostatization that mark it in the Targums and in the New Testament. Ben Sira had also referred to God's Word as the instrument of creation (42:15;43:5-10); but the idea of a separate agency is not fully developed. The close approximation of Wisdom to the Word that takes place in the Wisdom of Solomon has led some scholars to find the roots of the New Testament Logos doctrine in this Jewish development.[15]

Like Wisdom, in this book the Word is directly under God's control; it is integrally a part of him. In no wise is it an entity with an independent purpose, not an impersonal nationalistic or pantheistic force. So, in this also, this writer of Alexandria preserves the real genius of Jewish religion, despite his Hellenistic environment and the allurements to syncretism, to which Philo Judaeus would yield in a gen-

[15] Notably, Rendell Harris, *The Origin of the Prologue of St. John's Gospel* (Cambridge: At the University Press, 1917).

eration or two. Israel's wisdom movement was now a servant of its faith.

The equation of Wisdom with the concept of Spirit is another witness to its nationalization. This was a relationship with far-reaching results for religious development. We shall discuss it in a final chapter.

The Wisdom Literature following Pseudo-Solomon adds few new items to illustrate the process by which the Hebrew wisdom movement became an integral part of the religious heritage. It simply intensifies the factors already present. It represents, for the most part, documents written by passionate defenders of the Jewish faith and religious institutions. They are written to honor the martyrs and call the nation to steadfastness in dark days. The writers are the recognized custodians of the religious heritage, as well as the latter-day representatives of the wisdom movement. We cite three.

The Book of Baruch in the Apocrypha was probably written after A.D. 70, since it apparently presupposes the final destruction of the Temple (3:24; 4:10, 15, 33). The section that deals with wisdom is in two parts: the first reproaches the nation with the unfaithfulness that has produced its present plight, and the second gives a message of comfort for the future, which is almost a paraphrase of Isaiah, chapters 40–66 (3:9—4:4; 4:5—5:9). Israel is in captivity because she has forsaken the "spring of wisdom," which is the way of God. If she will but learn where wisdom is, she will find "life."

Then the question is answered. Wisdom is not the possession of the heathen or of their rulers. The rich do not have it. The ancient Edomites, so famed for wisdom, did not really have it. Nor did the Canaanites. Men cannot obtain wisdom by seeking for it. God, the Creator, alone knows it. This God who knows wisdom is "our God." He gave Wisdom to Israel alone. Wisdom came to earth and "mingled with men." It is none other than the Law which will endure forever. This Law is the hope of Israel's deliverance. Israel is the elect nation; she may suffer for her sins, but the gift of the eternal Law, symbol of God's merciful grace, is such that her name will be "called forever." This wisdom writer voices the intense religious and particularistic reaction produced by persecution. His hope for national survival is founded on his faith in the "grace" of God.

The Fourth Book of Maccabees probably appeared in Alexandria at the opening of the Christian era. It is a sermon that exhorts the persecuted to steadfastness and uses the Maccabean martyrs as examples. There are superficial accommodations to Hellenistic ideas. The standard Stoic virtues are cited. In conformity with neo-Platonic ideas the author also seems to place the center of evil in the human body rather than in the will, which would be more strictly Jewish (7:18; cf. Gal. 5:13).

But the writer is Jewish and believes that the Jew remains the light of the world, thanks to his national religious heritage. Wisdom is "the culture acquired under the Law." It may appear in the dress of Greek virtues (1:16–18); but at its heart lies a Jewish element, εὐσέβεια, which may be called "righteousness," "reverence," or "the fear of God" and which is an expression of faith in the eternal Law, which alone enables men to die as martyrs (5:23 f.; 15:29). Transcendent faith and religious nationalism are this writer's deepest motivations.

The Pirke Aboth is really a mishnaic tract of unusual quality and exhibits many of the features of Wisdom Literature. In literary character it is epigrammatic and frequently proverbial. As a homily on the Law it exhorts men to lean on the Law rather than on their own understanding (4:18). An epigram attributed to Rabbi Hanina ben Dosa well illustrates the manner in which the wisdom movement was fully assimilated by the Jewish religious tradition: "Everyone whose fear of sin precedes wisdom, his wisdom endures; and everyone whose wisdom precedes his fear of sin, his wisdom does not endure" (3:12). It is fitting to close this survey with a quotation from the rabbis; for the Hebrew wisdom movement, at first apparently unrelated to the national religious tradition, is finally submerged by and lost in rabbinism.

CHAPTER III

THE HOPE OF WISDOM

IN OUR first chapter we saw that the wisdom literature of the ancient cultures, which were the setting for the Hebrew wisdom movement, fell into two classes—the optimistic and the pessimistic. The former is world-affirming. It is assured that, despite his limitations, man can discover the nature of what determines his destiny to such an extent that he can obtain what he deems essential to his happiness. The latter despairs of this. The optimist is convinced that the world is governed by reason and morality. The rule is constant, and it is man's business to discover its character and to obey it. Thus he will become wise and able to determine his own destiny. The pessimist either doubts the existence of this rational and moral order or despairs of man's ability to discover its nature sufficiently well to guide him to a happy end. The former believes that, for all practical purposes, man can discover the ultimate norm by which life is tested and rewarded; the latter disbelieves this and may even deny the existence of the norm as a moral criterion.

These two classes also appear in the Hebrew Wisdom Literature. Job, Ecclesiastes, and Prov. 30:1-5 represent the second class—the tendency to despair. They will be dealt with later. In this chapter we shall examine the optimistic Hebrew Wisdom Literature. We must seek to understand what conception those who wrote it had of the norm that measures life, how they expected to learn to know it, and what rewards they expected for obeying it. Later we shall also see how the second, the despairing, tendency was an outgrowth of the optimistic view in the historical development of Jewish religion. We shall further examine the transcendent solution in which the process finally issued.

The classic Hebrew religious outlook of the prophets is world-affirming, and it is optimistic. Yahweh is sovereign, rational, and moral. His purposes and character are consistent and dependable and are revealed and realized in history. Those who obey Yahweh will be rewarded in this life, whether as individuals or in the social complex to which they belong. This hopeful faith is described as follows by Hilaire Duesberg: "Les vues foncières de l'Ancien Testament sur le monde sont résoluement optimistes; il ne doute pas que l'homme soit fait pour être heureux, ni qu'il ait été placé dans un univers parfaitement agencé par un Demiurge très puissant et très sage."[1]

Such an optimistic outlook, with its attendant doctrine of rewards, was also held by the wisdom writers to be considered in this chapter. In the beginning, however, their basis for it was rather different. To emphasize this contrast we shall first examine the prophetic teaching.

The prophetic doctrine of rewards in Israel was religious. A sovereign and moral God—"die heilige Verkörperung der ewigen sittlichen Idee"[2]—who was self-revealing controlled the rewards. Man's own experience of moral obligation and his application of this to the record of the past con-

[1] *Les Scribes inspirés: introduction aux livres sapientieux de la Bible*, II (2 vols.; Paris: Desclée de Brouwer, 1939), 6.

[2] Emil Balla, "Das Problem des Leides in der israelitisch-jüdischen Religion," *Euxaristeirion Hermann Gunkel* (Göttingen: Vandenhoek and Rupprecht, 1923), p. 225.

stituted the method by which the prophet arrived at his conception of the divine moral character. God was the prophet's own moral character, infinitely extended in purity, power, and time. There was a common element in the moral character of God and his prophets: the prophets also taught and influenced each other, together moving in a general direction. The Law, ever growing in bulk, was actually largely the applied record of these prophetic insights granted in the past. As it was further and further removed from the human experiences that produced it, it came to appear more and more transcendent in character.

This moral and dependable concept of deity developed by the prophets made optimism possible. Most primitive religions assume an element of caprice in their gods. The irrational behavior of the gods caused by jealousy or vengeance, or even by uncontrolled whims, makes the human lot terrifying and uncertain. We are reminded of the epigram, "Quem deus vult perdere, dementat prius." This could never be said of the moral Yahweh of the prophets. According to the prophets, man willed his own destruction.

There is evidence that this irrational and nonmoral quality had been present in pre-prophetic Hebrew conceptions: God hardened the pharaoh's heart (Exod. 7:3; Deut. 2:30); he makes David take a census (II Sam. 24:1); he moves Rheoboam to reject the counsel of the elders (I Kings 12: 15); and a spirit of Yahweh leads Ahab astray (I Kings 12:15). And then Yahweh "punishes" them all! Most of these are partially or completely moralized by later Hebrew writers for whom God has become moral. We notice especially that the divine refusal to permit Amaziah to listen to the wise counsel of Joash is explained by the specious argument that the people of Judah had sought the gods of Edom (II Chron. 25:18–22). Our present record still contains the account of Moses' circumcision without any moral explanation whatever (Exod. 4:24 f.). But for the Hebrew prophets the moral concept became supreme in their experience of God, and ideas of caprice were eliminated.

Faith in God's moral character and in man's ability to understand it was the real basis of Hebrew theodicy. All obedience to Yahweh is rewarded; all disobedience is punished. The Book of Deuteronomy was a legal work produced under the influence of the teaching of the prophets of the eighth century; its theory is that the entire national history should be interpreted on the basis of the doctrine of rewards.[3] If the nation will obey the Law of God, it will exercise hegemony over all peoples; its population will increase; the soil will yield abundantly; flocks and herds will multiply; and Israel will be "the head and not the tail" (Deut. 28:1–15). If the Law is disobeyed, the very opposite will happen: mankind, crops, and cattle will all be under a curse; disease and defeat by the enemy will produce the collapse of the national economy (28:15 ff.). The eschatology is historical, and the rewards are material; the motivation for obedience is both eudaemonistic and utilitarian. Such is the prophetic teaching about reward.

The historical writers applied this prophetic doctrine retroactively in interpreting their national history. All history was a record of God's acts, and the acts conformed to his character. The conception of this character held by the historians of the sixth century also became the yardstick

[3] O. S. Rankin, *Israel's Wisdom Literature: Its Bearing on Theology and the History of Religion* (Edinburgh: T. and T. Clark, 1936), p. 77.

by which to measure human behavior in an earlier era, in which men had held very different views of God's character and his demands upon them. This often confuses the actual facts of history. For example, we note the condemnation of the "high places" in periods long before the Josianic Reformation outlawed them (I Kings 3:2; 22:43; II Kings 12:3; 14:4; 15:4; 16:4). Similarly, in the Book of Judges, which repeatedly states the formula of sin and consequent disaster, the crucial sin is the worship of the be-ᶜalim and Astaroth (3:7; 10:6). Yet this was an aspect of syncretism which had probably hardly begun in the period of the settlement, though it became a great problem in the prophetic era.

Conversely, seeking to discover the nature and purpose of God by an analysis of history may often have given doubtful results for theology. Transferring the spirit and ideals of a people in a time of material prosperity to the divine character is still a very hazardous procedure! Describing their thought and practice in a period that brings material disaster as inimical to God's nature and purpose is equally dangerous. However, it is noteworthy that the prophetic historians never flinch from their own thesis. All comes to pass as it should. The final exile is the deserved fate of a rebellious people (II Kings 17:1–21). The so-called "Psalms of Innocence" must be explained by the same thesis. A book such as Job could have been produced only as a reaction against this dogma of a moral God who rewards men materially and on earth.

The later historians applied the doctrine of rewards to individuals as well as to the nation. This is one feature that distinguishes the Books of the Chronicles. For example, the writers of Kings report the virtues of Josiah and attribute his early and violent death to the sins of his fathers (II Kings 23:26); but the later writer of Chronicles accepts the theory that every disaster has its own proper antecedent sin. He probably also denies that sons are punished for the sins of the fathers. Hence, he produces a story that Josiah died because he sinned in his refusal to heed God's warning sent by Necho of Egypt (II Chron. 35:21 f.; cf. also II Kings 15:1–7 and II Chron. 26:16–24).

The factors producing this new doctrine of individualism are not easily ascertained. Ezekiel was probably the first to teach it explicitly. The national destruction and the Exile were factors that turned the people to individual concerns. The single person no longer found self-realization by living for and in a nation that was gradually becoming God's kingdom on earth. To think in terms of social solidarity now was depressing, for it implied atonement for the communal sins of the past. The slogan that every man would be punished for his own sin, preached by Ezekiel, was a word of encouragement.

The Wisdom Literature is almost entirely individualistic; but it is not likely that it influenced the development of individualism as a religious doctrine as early as the time of the Exile. The religious influence of the sages begins later.

In early Hebrew history God pays attention to individuals (Genesis, chaps. 24, 38; Exod. 4:24; II Sam. 3:39). Even with conceptions of intense social solidarity such as existed in ancient Israel, there is an inverted type of individualism. The social mass throws up some individual, who imposes his will on all and affects the entire society for good or ill. Tribal chieftains and modern "leaders" illustrate this; and in Israel the king played the role for the nation.

But the individualism which flowered at the time of the Exile contains moral responsibility as a new element. It is, in all probability, a result of prophetic influence. The prophets came to understand God and his way through the operation of their own experience and reason. God became known as a moral being in and through individual self-consciousness. This ennobled personality and made men personally and individually responsible.

Individual applications of the doctrine of rewards became much more difficult to justify. The Chronicler's account of Josiah shows this plainly. "I have been young, and now I am old; but I have not seen the righteous forsaken, nor his descendants begging their bread" (Ps. 37:25) is a generalization that cannot long go unchallenged. Job does not find it justifiable; but he is not the only doubter, or even the first; prophets and psalmists were also frequently bewildered and confused by it (Jer. 12:1 ff.; Ps. 44:17–19).

To meet this growing difficulty with the doctrine of rewards, extant corollaries to it were emphasized and new ones were introduced. For example, trouble might be probationary, God's way of testing a man's loyalty. So Judg. 2:22–3:6 accounts for the failure of Israel to annihilate the Canaanites (cf. Genesis, chap. 22; Job, chaps. 1, 2). By steadfastness, one's faith would ultimately be vindicated and rewarded. Then there was also the corollary doctrine that trouble might be disciplinary, a brief punishment for the minor lapses into which all fall—a punishment designed to teach men God's way more clearly and so enable them to share more fully in the goodness of life (Pss. 94:12 f.; 119: 66 f.). A wider view of this, presupposing social interdependence and responsibility, is presented in Second Isaiah. In the Servant Songs it introduces the element of vicariousness; the troubles of the "servant" are a punishment for the sins of others. Yet the doctrine of rewards is not abrogated. Transgression still implies the forfeiture of material good (Isa. 48:17–19). The reward of the servant, whatever its nature, will be greater because of his service (53:10–12).

A much more radical change produced by the difficulty in applying the doctrine of rewards individually consisted in separating the religious from the eudaemonistic side of life. This abolished the expectation of any material reward for religious obedience—obedience was its own reward. This change really went to the root of the problem, since the basic difficulty with the doctrine of rewards was that there was no organic relation between the moral law obeyed and the material rewards expected. The only logical reward for moral obedience would have to consist in an immediate participation in the moral purpose that evoked obedience, that is, the only true reward would consist in God's gift of his own character to those who obeyed him (Hab. 3:17–19; Ps. 73:23–28). This teaching was too exalted and "spiritual" to make great appeal to the ancient Hebrews. One wonders how much better it fares today.

Our review of the prophetic doctrine of rewards has been rather extensive; but it may help us to understand a bit more clearly the peculiarities of the similar doctrine taught in the optimistic Wisdom Literature. The difference in the doctrine in the prophetic and the wisdom traditions is often referred to the so-called "prudential" character of the rewards sought by the sages. But this is doubtful. In its emphasis upon material rewards the prophetic tradition is also prudential. If the sages move on a low religious plane because they are interested in the "fruits" of their obedience, it follows that in this respect the prophets share their stature. It seems that the difference between the doctrines of reward in the two traditions is much better explained by tracing it back to the divergent manner in which the prophets and the sages conceived of arriving at an understanding of the way of life that would bring rewards—that is, the difference grows out of different ideas held about revelation. The prophets were very subjective; hence discovery of truth for them rested on the conviction that man and God lived in intimate fellowship by virtue of a common moral consciousness. God took the initiative and disclosed himself in human awareness. The applied records of this disclosure became a transcendent divine Law. The religious outlook is a vertical one: God speaks to the experience of the prophet; the latter, applying God's ''word,'' announces his demands to the people. The sages are objective; they study the way of life in nature and history. The subjective activity of God recedes. Their outlook is a horizontal one; hence their ethical teaching appears less religious than that of the prophets.

To clarify our discussion of the doctrine of rewards in the Wisdom Literature, we must note that it uses the term ''wisdom'' in four distinct ways. (1) Wisdom may mean an individual's understanding of life and the rules he has obtained by the use of all his natural endowments, mental and physical (Prov. 17:24; 10:13; 11:12; 21:30). Thus a man whose understanding and insight are true is a wise man. (2) Wisdom may also refer to the accumulated lore of the past, the rules for life and living produced by the sages and taught to successive generations (Prov. 1:1–6; Ben Sira 8:8; 39:1–30). (3) Wisdom is an element in God, an eternal and divine possession, the divine intelligence, created from before the beginning and never wholly comprehensible by man (Ben Sira 1:1, 4, 6). (4) Finally, wisdom may be a special divine gift granted by God to men, subsequent to and apart from their creation. Therefore, it is not a result of their use of their natural faculties, but a special grace (Prov. 8:22 ff.; Ben Sira, chap. 24; Wisd. of Sol. 7:22 ff.; Bar. 4:1 f.).

The degree and manner of relationship between these four expressions of wisdom is of central importance in arriving at an understanding of the relation between the wisdom concept and the doctrine of the Spirit. The way in which these manifestations of wisdom are brought together indicates how the wisdom movement thought about revelation, for it is its way of dealing with the perennial tensions of human freedom and divine transcendence. The details of the relationship will be taken up later; but it must be said immediately that, whether it be the hidden divine intelligence or man's "secular" possession, wisdom is all of one piece in the ancient world. Each of the myths of the Tree of Knowledge, Prometheus, and Ea illustrates this in its own manner. In the Book of Proverbs, chapters 1–9, the Divine Wisdom, operating in creation and now inviting men to possess it, is in full rapport with human prudence.

The Jewish sages teach a doctrine of rewards similar to that of the prophets (Prov. 1:33; 3:1; 10:3, 6, 24, 27–30; Ben Sira 12:2; 40:15; Wisd. of Sol. 6:10). Hugo Gressmann and others think they originated the doctrine in Israel; but it seems impossible to answer this question conclusively. In any event their acceptance of the doctrine presupposes their conviction that the world is morally governed. In teaching the reward doctrine the sages are individualistic in their emphasis. Each one is charged to find God's way for himself; and each one is individually responsible for his deeds. Where there is a group emphasis, it is more often upon a class within the nation, such as wise or fools, upright or wicked, than upon the nation as a whole. Wisdom and righteousness consist in the common virtues that build a healthy society: sober speech (Prov. 12:18; 15: 4), forbearance (14:29), honesty (12:17), self-control (17: 27), industry (12:24), intelligence (12:8), humaneness (12:10), good will (14:22), patience (15:18), philanthropy (14:21), tractableness (15:5), reverence (10:27), justice (16:8), modesty (18:2), humility (16:9), and fidelity (5:15 ff.). The list can be extended almost indefinitely. In a later era, when the Law becomes the norm for wisdom, its contents form the prescription for the good life.

Like the prophets, the older wisdom documents limit their eschatological outlook to life on earth, which is the arena of life's rewards. All desirable rewards the sages frequently sum up in the word "life" (Prov. 10:16 f.; 11:4, 30; 15:24; 16:22; cf. also Deut. 30:15 ff.), while the word is sometimes equated with the word "health." The content of these terms is spiritualized in the later Wisdom of Solomon; but even in Proverbs there are cases where this is true (3:18; 8:19).

Normally, however, the rewards are material and eudaemonistic in the older writings. The obedient will possess the land in wealth and honor (Prov. 1:33; 10:4, 30). The wise and good will live long, but the wicked die young (Prov. 12:28; Ben Sira, chap. 20). The numerous posterity of the obedient will flourish (Prov. 12:3, 7, 12). The memory of the good endures after death (Prov. 10:7), and their grandchildren will possess their heritage (Prov. 13:22). The wise

enjoy "peace" and health (Ben Sira 1:18); good men are
their faithful friends (Ben Sira 3:17); and they will enjoy
the favor and love of God, be praised for their understanding, and finally judge the heathen (Ben Sira 39:9)! In this
list of rewards one misses the frequent reference to the fertility of the flocks and herds and the soil, which is the reward so often singled out by the prophetic writers. The
prophets probably addressed more popular congregations,
made up of people directly concerned with these matters.
The sages moved and taught in circles far removed from the
soil and despaired of the farmer as a subject for wisdom
(Ben Sira 38:25–27). Yet we do find the more delicate assertion that a recognition of God as the giver of the fruit of the
soil will increase its abundance (Prov. 3:4 f.).

Though the rewards in the Wisdom of Solomon are no
longer chiefly material and temporal, these are not wholly
excluded. This is particularly true of the latter half of the
book. Rankin considers this part of the book a rabbinic ap-
pendix added to emphasize that God's moral order is also
operative in history and rewards men on earth as well as in
the hereafter. He feels that those who added chapters 10–19
wished to counteract the apocalyptic tendency of the earlier
part of the book.[4] Whatever the merits of this view, it must
not be permitted to obscure the fact that the earlier chapters
also contain a temporal and utilitarian note about rewards
(6:25; 8:7).

But the real rewards in the Wisdom of Solomon, whether
in this life or beyond, are spiritual. The greatest reward of
all is immortality (1:15; 2:23; 13:7), which includes
"peace," rest with God, and his protection (3:3; 4:7;

[4] *Ibid.*, p. 114.

5:17). In this life wisdom brings keen judgment, a blameless life, and knowledge of God and of what pleases him (4:9; 8:11; 9:18); it also rewards its possessor with the four virtues of self-control, courage, understanding, and righteousness (8:7). By wisdom a man can understand the true significance of natural science (7:16 ff.). And for the nation wisdom provides national deliverance (chaps. 10 ff.). Wisdom makes men friends of God, and in the eschatological reign the righteous and wise will share in his rule and judge the nations (3:8; 5:16; 6:21).

Those who scorn and reject wisdom receive an opposite set of rewards in the Wisdom of Solomon. They invite death, which God had never intended for earth (1:12, 16). Their wives are silly, their children evil, and their old age unhonored (3:12, 17). Among the dead they are punished forever (4:19). There seems to be no contemplation of the resurrection of the wicked. The greatest punishment of the wicked on earth is their inability to see the good (4:12); after death it is their rejection at the last judgment (3:18; 4:20; 5:16 ff.).

It is sometimes asserted rather easily that the writers of the optimistic Wisdom Literature were not troubled by, or aware of, doubt about the validity of the doctrine of reward. Cheyne feels that this is true of Ben Sira: ". . . . he really seems no more troubled by doubts of this ancient doctrine than the author of the beautiful but in many respects naively simple Book of Proverbs."[5] Such remarks would be true if one were to limit the evidence to explicit expressions of doubt, which are not found; but Ben Sira's urgent appeals to those who were in doubt are ample evidence

[5] T. K. Cheyne, *Job and Solomon* (New York: Thomas Whittaker, 1893), p. 189.

that he was keenly aware of the problem, possibly in spite of himself (2:10 ff.; 16:13–23). Even the Book of Proverbs may not be so "naïvely simple" on this point as is intimated; it declares the wages of the wicked to be "illusive" (11: 18, 21, 23). Such protest indicates awareness of the problem. The God who was to be trusted could not be wholly understood (Prov. 20:24). This aggravated the problem and ultimately produced the pessimistic wisdom writings. The Wisdom of Solomon is essentially a reply to those who doubt or deny that the wise and upright are remembered by God (2:1 ff.; 5:4 ff.).

The corollaries to the doctrine of reward, which we noted in the prophetical tradition and which explained the trouble of the virtuous, also occur in the wisdom writings. The wise and righteous may be in trouble because God is testing them: good metal must be tried by fire (Prov. 17:3; 27:21). The scorners apply this method themselves in the Wisdom of Solomon (2:19). So God tries his own, and they are made perfect (3:6; 4:16). This illumines the statement of Jesus in Matt. 6:1 f. Those who had reward here would have none beyond. In the Wisdom of Solomon all life on earth is probationary; for the upright, trouble has become a mark of the divine favor—it indicates that they are being prepared for heaven.

The disciplinary theory of trouble is also used by the wise. All have some sin (Prov. 20:9). The punishment of the faithful is comparable to that of the son by the father who loves him (Prov. 3:11 f.; 11:31; 13:24; Ben Sira 4:17; Wisd. of Sol. 3:5; 11:9).

The complete separation of the religious and eudaemonistic motives made but little headway in the central Jewish

religious tradition. It receives scant attention in the earlier
Wisdom Literature. Proverbs thinks of wisdom as a possession to be valued for its own sake. It is the "crown" of the
wise and more to be prized than "corals" (8:11; 14:24; cf.
also Ben Sira 4:17 f.). But this is almost the only disinterested note we find.

In the later period of the movement it is difficult to determine how great the role of disinterested religion was. The
constant invocation of future rewards complicates the problem. Bousset thinks that any intimation that virtue was
its own reward was purely accidental.[6] Schechter, on the
contrary, considers it a normative conception and feels that
the motive of doing a thing "purely for the love of God"
was powerful enough among the nobler minds of Israel to
enable them "to dispense utterly with the motives of reward and punishment."[7] This is certainly an extreme assertion. The Pirke Aboth does contain some passages that
inculcate a disinterested piety (1:3; 2:16; 4:2); but it also
contains passages that indicate that the virtuous normally
expected some reward in addition to virtue (2:1, 7, 19). In
IV Maccabees, Eleazer asserts that even if it were true, as
Antiochus maintains, that the Law for which he is about to
die is not divine, he would still be bound to obey it since it
is the law of his land. It would be wrong for him to destroy
his people's reputation for piety (5:16–18), that is, Eleazer
is ready to die for honor, if need be. Yet his actual motiva-

[6] Wilhelm Bousset, *Die Religion des Judentums im späthellenistischen Zeitalter*, ed. Hugo Gressmann (Tübingen: J. C. B. Mohr, 1926), p. 145.

[7] Solomon Schechter, *Some Aspects of Rabbinic Theology* (New York: Macmillan Co., 1909), p. 169.

tion is by no means so disinterested as that, for the sermon he preaches is voluble about the reward of the faithful after death (IV Macc. 10:15; 13:17; 17:4, 18). Conversely, his persecutors will receive punishment (9:8, 32; 10:11, 15; 12:19).

The account of vicarious suffering, which does not necessarily dispense with the idea of reward, scarcely occurs in the early Wisdom Literature. Proverbs and Ben Sira are hardly aware that the cost of righteousness may be very great. This enhances their prudential reputation and makes the vicarious element superfluous. Proverbs cautions the wise not to obligate himself too deeply to his fellows (17: 18; 27:13); it is foolish to spend one's effort trying to help fools. It does ask the wise to rescue those being led away to an unjust execution (24:11). And one must feed one's enemy and not return evil for a transgression; but here the motives are scarcely vicarious (25:21 f.). Ben Sira asks men to become responsible for widows and orphans (4:1). Altogether, the idea that the establishment of truth may cost a great price is not realized.

This is very different in the later wisdom writings. IV Maccabees is perhaps the best testimony to this (6:28; 17: 22). In the Wisdom of Solomon the writer is also aware of the great cost of righteousness. The upright, he finds, is persecuted for having sought to point out the errors of the wicked. He is put to death by them so that they may see if his assertion that he is a "son of God" is well founded; for, of course, if he is, God will rescue him (2:12–20; cf. Matt. 27:42 ff.). LaGrange feels that the notion of a messiah as a vicarious sufferer was greatly furthered by this document. He refers to the passage just cited as "une véritable pro-

phétie de la Passion du Sauveur."[8] It must be remembered
that in this later period the prophetic and wisdom traditions were more and more blended; it is no longer quite possible to refer to any specific element as the sole development
of either the one or the other.

We have seen that the optimistic sages, like the representatives of prophetic religion, believed that life was lived
against the background of a moral, rational order. They were
convinced that they must conform to this order. The character of this order was similarly defined by both groups;
consequently, the rules for living were very similar. And,
except for the changes brought about by the new eschatological outlook, in which the later Wisdom Literature
shares, the rewards expected are very similar.

We must now see how the sages thought to obtain wisdom. How had they obtained the knowledge of God's character that they possessed and on which their rules for happiness were based?

We note, first, that the sages were all convinced that not
all men were equally capable of obtaining wisdom. Men
were all God's creatures; but they differed profoundly; some
were wise, others foolish; some were righteous and some
wicked. The sages apparently felt that there were predes-
tined elements that determined these groups. Environmen-
tal factors do not account for the distinctions; nor, perhaps,
does natural mental equipment by itself—but that is more
problematical.

The sages do not contemplate the possibility of conversion; they doubt that a man actually wicked or foolish can

[8] M. J. LaGrange, "Le Livre de la sagesse; sa doctrine des fins dernières," *Revue
biblique*, VII (1907), 98.

become righteous or wise. Fools scorn wisdom (Prov. 1:7, 32); scoffers delight in scoffing (Prov. 1:22); and it is wasted effort to attempt to teach them (Prov. 9:7). Those who are without wisdom do not appreciate its value; nor are they aware of their own poverty (Prov. 13:19); hence they do not want wisdom. Foolishness and wickedness so blind men that it is impossible for them to discern wisdom, even if they do desire it (Prov. 14:6; 17:16; Ben Sira 15:7; Wisd. of Sol. 2:21 f.; 4:12). Foolishness and evil are progressive (Prov. 14:8). Their victims are unable to see where their road leads (Prov. 4:19). It seems that God has intended that some men should be foolish (Prov. 24:7). The wicked, who may differ slightly from the foolish in the early strata of Proverbs, cannot receive wisdom (Wisd. of Sol. 10:4 ff.). Wisdom does invite even the foolish; their possibility of repentance depends upon an early response (Prov. 9:4 f.). It is easily understood why the wisdom teachers were chiefly concerned with the training of the young; wisdom was a process of development which paralleled the natural development of physical existence.

The same double emphasis occurs in Ben Sira. All men are created in God's image; all have understanding and the natural capacity for wisdom; but not all become wise. Men know the distinction between good and evil by virtue of their creation; they are endowed with reason and a mind with which to think; they have their natural senses with which to read the meaning of life in the phenomenal world about them (17:1-9). There seems to him to be an immanent moral law, which is a universal human endowment (17:12) and gives man natural wisdom. In addition, the Divine Wisdom lived among men from the beginning; it was created with the "faithful" in the womb (1:10, 14 f.). Thus some seem to have a special gift for Divine Wisdom from the very beginning, in addition to the natural intelligence with which all men are endowed. Ben Sira, by invoking Divine Wisdom as a special gift for some persons, has an explanation for the natural differences in people that Proverbs also observed.

We see that, each in its own way, the Book of Proverbs and Ben Sira balance human freedom against structural determinism and/or divine initiative of an elective sort. Universality and election are held in a tension that steers midway between the naturalistic free will of the Sadducees and the fatalism of the Essenes. We are reminded of the dictum in the Pirke Aboth: "All is foreseen, but freedom of choice is given" (3:14). For Ben Sira the tension seems to produce no conflict. God had chosen Israel. The Law had been offered to others but rested in Israel. Now he also sees an individual election. Some Jews were peculiarly chosen of God; and some non-Jews were similarly chosen (33:12).

The earliest wisdom writers recognized predetermined handicaps and advantages. The sages offer no explanation for these; nor do they serve as an excuse for failing to seek wisdom. Whatever natural human equipment a man had was his instrument for the acquisition of wisdom. Human freedom, a pioneering spirit, and an unprejudiced approach are characteristic of the earlier records of the sages. Confidence in man's natural, creaturely ability is at its highest. This explains the almost complete lack of the attribute of mercy already noted in the previous chapter. Mercy in God indicates a loss of human self-confidence about the capacity to discover and fulfil the demands of God. The earliest wisdom writers still expected to find the way and the means of following it.

How was this to be accomplished? Proverbs assumes that wisdom is to be found all about one, both in men and in the material processes of life. To find wisdom one must use one's eye to see what goes on in the world (3:21; 17:24; 27:12); one should even study natural life (6:6; 8:34; 30:24–28); and one must keep one's ears alert to hear all that men say (2:2; 18:15; 28:19). Having done this, one must sort out and evaluate the results, applying the mind in evaluating discernment (5:1; 7:3; 18:15; 22:17; 23:12).

To obtain wisdom, the desire to have it must always remain uppermost. To seek to know the order by which one is ruled and by which one must live must be the focal point of life to which all else pays tribute (2:4; 8:17; 15:14). It must be an eager all-consuming search inspired by a desire to be able to distinguish the right from the wicked way, the wise from the foolish. This ability constitutes the possession of truth; it is to be valued above all else (23:23). The eager confidence and the elevated goal of these early sages compels admiration—they were strong characters.

There are further special forms that the search for wisdom may take. A person may study the accumulated lore of wisdom—the proverbs, which are a common possession and some of which have been written down by the wise. The young must heed the instruction of parents (13:1). Conversation with the wise produces understanding. The discourses of the wise, their counsel, their maxims, and their instruction are to be heeded (3:1; 4:10, 20; 5:7; 10:17; 13:14, 18; 19:20, 27). The entire process of obtaining wisdom, as we see it reflected in the early wisdom materials, is one of complete freedom and objectivity. No national or institutional barriers are set up. There is no designated body of material, already extant and delimited, which is definitive for the search. At least in the very earliest material, the wisdom seeker must rely entirely on his natural human equipment. Proverbs, chapters 10–31, does not hint at any divine initiative of wisdom, much less at the granting of wisdom under one form or another as a special gift, to enable man to find it more easily.

As means of obtaining wisdom, divine initiative and special divine grace are first encountered in the latest section of the Book of Proverbs. Here not only does man seek for wisdom; Wisdom herself seeks man. Wisdom wants to teach men. To all she issues a free invitation; those who desire her will discover her (1:20–23, 32; 8:1 ff., 32). If one took this language entirely metaphorically, one could say that this was merely the sage's poetic way of saying that a man who really wishes to become wise and uses all his natural endowments zealously would certainly discover wisdom for himself. More probably, however, it means that the sage felt that there was a self-revealing aspect to the very order whose nature he was trying to understand. This self-revealing aspect is the Divine Wisdom, which is described as eternal, formed before the world, and present at its creation (8:22 f.).

Thus Divine Wisdom takes the initiative. In part man's search for wisdom becomes receptivity. Yet, at this point, it does not cut short or make impossible man's use of the natural methods to which he had at first been limited and does not in any way disparage man's natural intellectual faculties; it is rather conceived as being the impulse that makes them operative in a certain way. Nor is this Divine Wisdom here identified with the Mosaic Law, though that was to be true later on. It does not express itself in terms of a gift to any special nation or group; neither does it close areas of search to men seeking wisdom. Yet this reference to the divine initiative as an indispensable aid to man in his search for the divine way is a new note. It marks the beginning of a process which parallels the nationalization of the Hebrew wisdom movement and influences it as profoundly. To this we shall return later.

If there was no recognition of a divine initiative in the earlier strata of Proverbs, no special aid from God to enable man to become wise, did the writers who produced them have a really religious understanding of life? It seems quite obvious that this literature manifests no great affective devotion and enthusiasm for the divine, and the writers reveal no deep personal experience of religious truth. Unlike the prophets, the early sages of Israel did not find their way to an understanding of their world and its God by way of an inner experience of personal moral relationship to God in which God takes the initiative. How, then, did they look at life? Were they entirely "humanistic" and "secular" in the sense that they felt that they determined their own destiny by means of their own discovery and doctrine, without reference to an objective moral order? Did they leave religion out of sight in this sense? It is a frequent assertion that they did.

Hermann Gunkel is one of those who insist that, in the beginning, Hebrew Wisdom Literature was entirely secular in the sense that it was opportunistic rather than concerned with moral principles.[9] He feels that the sages were, at

[9] "Vergeltung," in *Die Religion in Geschichte und Gegenwart* . . . . (Tübingen: J. C. B. Mohr, 1927).

first, not in search of the character of a rational cosmic order by which they believed life to be governed, but they merely tried to get along by seeing what worked best for them. He insists that the religious motive was introduced later by uniting the belief in the worth of wisdom as prudential lore with the belief in God as Judge—that is, opportunistic prudence was baptized and became morality.

To evaluate this assertion is very difficult, since it is almost impossible to discover the earlier origins of the material that now comprises chapters 10–29 of the Book of Proverbs. But we have tried to look at these chapters in the light of Gunkel's theory.

Earlier we saw that it was characteristic of wisdom writers to set men in opposite classes, with the qualities and fate of men in each class put down in direct contrast to those of its opposite. This is repeated again and again. The brief parallelisms of the older section of Proverbs are often antithetical and are used for this contrast of the classes. Two pairs of classes are thus developed. The first pair sets the wicked over against the righteous, this contrast being made no less than thirty-four times in chapters 10–15 alone. To this must be added the four times that the wicked are contrasted to the upright. The second pair of conflicting classes developed and set over against each other are the wise and the fools, to the latter of which we may add the scoffers. This pair is set in contrast fourteen times in the first six chapters, and the contrast continues throughout.

The positive and negative members of each of these two pairs of opposites have much in common. In a sense they complement each other and might be called synonymous; yet there are discernible differences. These appear when we

examine the context in which each is used. "Righteous"
and "wicked" are terms used to characterize persons whose
conduct is evaluated chiefly in terms of morality and religion. Their use is nearly always accompanied by a reference
to Yahweh. Basic principles of morality are stressed and
ultimate rewards count for most. In the case of the terms
"fools" and "wise," there is no explicit denial of the values on the basis of which the "wicked" and the "righteous"
are separated. Yet this pair of opposites is applied to persons on the basis of whether they are or are not mentally
alert and willing to learn. Yahweh is never mentioned.
Could this contrast offer a clue to the evidence substantiat-
ing Gunkel's assertion? Is the material using the terms
"wise" and "fool" older than that which uses "wicked"
and "righteous"? And is it wholly lacking in religious
awareness? A small amount of "crossing" has already taken
place (10:18, 21; 14:9). This, little though it is, re-empha-
sizes the fact that the earlier history of these materials is
lost in obscurity. It is so difficult to rediscover how and
when they were produced and brought together into their
present form that it becomes impossible to deal conclusively
with Gunkel's assertion. Yet the possible evidence for it
seems suggestive.

Perhaps the greatest argument against Gunkel's theory
that the Hebrew wisdom movement became religious at a
relatively late date is the objection that this would comport
rather badly with the movement's setting amid the older
wisdom movements of the Orient, its relation to them and
dependence upon them. A religious note occurs frequently
in the Egyptian wisdom literature. God's scrutinizing om-
niscience, his control of human destinies, and his role of

Judge are stressed, even in such ancient documents as Ptahhotep and the Instruction for King Merikere.

Whatever may have been the character of the Hebrew
movement before the composition of the oldest sections of
the Book of Proverbs as we have it now, these remains show
us an outlook that may be termed religious. This, we feel,
is true despite the fact that, according to them, man carries
on his search for wisdom unaided by any divine initiative
or special gift. This material reflects what may be called a
religious view of life because in it man recognizes his creaturehood. His whole life, including the rational faculties
with which he sought wisdom, was a divine endowment.
Man is thought of as a creature.

The success of man's search for wisdom depended upon his
possession of the "fear of Yahweh" (10:27; 14:26 f.; 15:16,
33; 16:16; 19:23). The term is described as the "discipline"
of Yahweh, that which keeps the search for wisdom on the
right path (15:33). Pride and insolence are typical of those
who lack this fear (15:25; 21:24). Fear of the Lord brings
riches, honor, and life; it is a fountain of life, insuring
length of days and security to one's children. These are
equivalent to the characteristic rewards of wisdom for
which it is a prerequisite even in these early sections of
Proverbs. We have previously indicated that the phrase is a
humble acknowledgment by man that he cannot possess
wisdom as God does. This is also true in the early strata of
Proverbs (15:11; 20:24; 24:12; 29:13).

The oldest parts of Proverbs teach that man discovers
wisdom; but it likewise feels that the roots of wisdom are
fixed in the God who is man's Creator. God makes both the
laws and the men who discover them. In the early stage of

the wisdom movement here represented, God does not give man wisdom, or any key to it, as a special gift; instead, he gives all men wisdom potentially, as a part of the order of creation. There is no "special gift of grace"; but life itself, with all its endowments, is a gift.

The early sages do not ask men to put away foreign gods, as the prophets do, or to bring their sacrifices, as the priests do. They ask men to use their faculties and their reason and to heed the conscience, which is the voice of God in the human soul. The wisdom which natural man discovers empirically is, by virtue of man's creaturehood, related to the divine in the sequence of effect and cause.

The earliest strata of Proverbs are "secular" in the sense that they apply what they have discovered about life to all human situations. The earliest sages are "humanists" because they seek wisdom as natural men, unaided by special divine initiative. But they are also "religious," for they are conscious of living as creatures in an order of creation whose controlling intelligence is their Judge. Their manner of obtaining wisdom differs from that of the prophets. Since there is no divine initiative supplementing creation, there is no word of God beyond that given by human reason; and the deliverances of reason are not called the "word" of God. Since there is no deep awareness of the national tradition and because there is confidence that a reverent and diligent use of one's natural faculties will teach a man all he needs to know to find "life," there is no mercy. Revelation is wholly natural; but an element of mystery remains. Man does not discover all, for man is a creature.

As the Hebrew wisdom movement progressed, it lost its

earlier creative urge. The free, pioneering spirit gave way to caution. The nationalization of the movement limited the search for wisdom to religiously prescribed channels. It is also possible that the slackening of the urge to search and discover truth produced a greater and too fearful respect for the admonition that the fear of Yahweh was wisdom. We seem to notice a mark of this in the second chapter of the Book of Proverbs. It is a chapter which advocates a restless and determined search for wisdom by man. But verses 5–8 are, it seems, an interpolation that breaks this theme and cautions that God is the giver of wisdom.

As a means by which to acquire wisdom, natural human faculties fall more and more into disuse in the later period. In Ben Sira the use of eye, ear, and mind still plays a diminished role; later it drops out still more. The earlier admonition to seek the counsel and companionship of the wise also decreases. Instead of seeking the wise, men are told to seek wisdom, that is, that body of material which is normative. This is usually the equal of the Law. Thus the movement recedes from the full immediacy of life and experience, and the search for wisdom is replaced by the prayer for it (Wisd. of Sol. 7:7; 9:1 f.).

As the human search recedes, emphasis upon the divine initiative grows. All counsel comes by the wisdom which is God's gift. Wisdom is given in the Law or in some other form of the national religious heritage. It becomes a special gift of God, given rather than discovered. It is no longer a part of the order of creation. This belongs to the transcendence of wisdom and its significance will be discovered in chapter iv.

CHAPTER IV

THE TRANSCENDENCE OF WISDOM

EVEN the optimistic Hebrew wisdom writers are always mindful that man is a creature who depends upon his creator, and it is thus that they account for human frailty and ignorance. Man cannot plumb the motives by which he is judged (Prov. 16:2); man's hopes fail because he cannot see the end from the beginning; the very course of his life is already planned (Prov. 16:25; 20:24). The divine purpose crushes his own (Prov. 19:21; Ben Sira 6:2; 7:11). Man cannot control his environment (Ben Sira 27:1), since God's status as creator makes it impossible for him to reveal all things (Prov. 25:2; Ben Sira 1:1–3). Even the human equipment with which wisdom is discovered is a divine gift (Prov. 29:13). Therefore, the point of departure for the wisdom seeker is the almighty God, his creator. In the final analysis, since a man cannot fully know, he can only believe that the world in which he lives and works is part of a rationally and morally governed order; for "his ways are from Yahweh" (Prov. 24:24).

The earliest strata of Proverbs and Job and Ecclesiastes all seek to understand the nature of life by means of man's natural endowments. The difference is that the first is confident that enough of this way can be discovered to enable men to earn happiness, while the last two despair of it. All limit themselves to natural means in the search for the true norm of life and insist that the results be confirmed in life's experience. Faith and grace are limited to the level of the order of creation.

When this natural-empirical method seems to fail, the only alternative to despair is a transcendent faith. That alternative is followed in the conclusion of the Job dialogue. Job, chapter 23, is probably the last authentic chapter. The poet feels that God is transcendent, but moral and just, and that suffering is the lot of all. He has faith that God's justice will be revealed to the righteous and vindicate them, probably in She'ol and through a mediator.[1] Ecclesiastes chooses the former alternative out of what seems to be the dead end of the natural-empirical method; it ends in despair.

When, as in Job, the recourse is to a transcendent faith, man may be content to rest and trust in ignorance, simply living in hope. This Job seems to do. More probably, however, this transcendent faith will fix upon some historical institution, document, or personality as an authoritative "given" means for discovering the way of life or as the very embodiment of that way. Such a given means is then a special gift, a gift in the order of grace. The Hebrew wisdom movement's recognition of human creaturehood conditioned it from the beginning to enter either the path of despair or the path of faith and grace.

This dilemma of Israel's wisdom movement can be stated in still another manner: All wisdom is God's possession, and its acquisition makes man, in some measure, divine. Complete possession of wisdom by man would entail his complete control over his destiny and his full equation with

[1] William A. Irwin, "An Examination of the Progress of Thought in the Dialogue of Job," *Journal of Religion*, XIII (1933), 150 ff.

deity, which would have been a blasphemous thought for the sages, even for the most "secular." Recognizing an order of creation, as they do, human ability and initiative ever contend with divine transcendence. Hence, Ecclesiastes despairs; Job must live by faith.

In their challenge to the classic doctrine of rewards, Job and Ecclesiastes reflect an attitude that was not uncommon in post-Exilic Judaism in its more orthodox forms. Religion was in reaction from the high confidence that marked the return from the Exile. Documents such as Haggai, Zechariah, Isaiah, chapters 56–66, and Malachi all illustrate this. In Judaism the later prophecy, apocalypticism, and legalism all pursued a course of transcendent faith and grace. The pre-Exilic prophetism, which looked for divine revelation in immediate and individual human experience, had faded out. It is not improbable that their detachment from the religious tradition helps to explain why Job and Ecclesiastes did not choose the way of special grace, be it Law or priest or Spirit. In any case they represent the last efforts of self-reliance.

We may begin an analysis of the despairing view of Job and Ecclesiastes by noting the very sharp and frequent contrast they make between the positions of God and of man. The greatness of God was in itself no new theme for the wise, and Proverbs frequently dwells on it. God is the creator of the world and of man with his faculties (3:19 f.); he is almighty, omniscient, and omnipresent (15:3, 11; 16:9; 17:3; and *passim*); he is the master of men's thoughts and deeds—all things contribute to his purpose. In Proverbs all this reinforces man's optimism and his conviction that he lives in an orderly world; but in Job and Ecclesiaste sit breeds humility or despair by confirming ever more deeply the inscrutability of God. Job and Ecclesiastes are in despair because they feel that human capacity is unable to bridge the gap between man and such an exalted deity and because they refuse to yield to irrational and unverifiable concepts of faith and grace.

In the Book of Job the friends, who represent the optimistic position, still view God's great power as a boon, and they insist that it secures the certainty of reward. He who sends the rain and controls the elements frustrates the crafty and brings to an end the counsel of schemers (5:9 ff.). This great, beneficent power keeps man alive (33:4 f.; 34:14); his greatness insures his benevolence (35:5-8). God's holy might should not frighten men but should humble them and remind them that no one is wholly free from sin.

But Job himself is thrown into doubt and confusion because God does not seem to be true to the moral character which men ascribe to him. His might is frightening. How can he, a mere man, debate with this one who stretches out the heavens, overturns mountains, and walks upon the billows (9:2-10)? It is precisely God's greatness that makes Job discouraged. Surely, God controls his lot; he stands behind all that has happened, for he is the master of life (12: 9-10, 13, 25).

But why did things happen as they did? What in God's nature demanded the events that have taken place? Unless Job knows this, he is without compass, and God's might is sheer terror. He cannot even begin to obey unless he knows the way. Hitherto he had always believed that he knew God well enough to understand his duty; but apparently he did not. Therefore, he now wishes to "speak" with God

(9:2 f., 14 f., and *passim*). He must discover new elements in God that will explain his present situation. How does he hope to come by it? Does he expect a "revelation" not the product of his own natural faculties yet verifiable in experience and in the rewards of life that result from obeying it? We are not told. But for Job the discovery of this new element is much more important than the recovery of his property; for, unless the nature of the Almighty's moral rule can be known, life has lost all meaning.

It is clear that the driving concern of the dialogue of Job is to maintain some moral interpretation of life with its attendant doctrine of reward. O. S. Rankin feels that its net result is merely to re-emphasize the disciplinary value of trouble.[2] In so far as this is true, the book fails in its purpose. H. W. Hertzberg feels that the book wants to lay bare the "Primitivität" and "Unmöglichkeit" of the doctrine of reward taught by the sages;[3] but it must be noted that the argument assumes God's moral governance of the temporal world in which men live and work. He neither presents nor asks for another form of the doctrine of rewards. He must know God better; all modifications in the doctrine will depend on hitherto undiscovered understanding of God; but he fears that God's greatness will make it impossible for him to learn the truth about his nature and way.

The writer of Ecclesiastes is also aware of God's greatness (3:11, 14 f.; 8:17; 11:5). Man's life is a gift of God (8:15; 9:9; 12:7); God ordains both good and evil (6:2; 7:14).

---

[2] *Israel's Wisdom Literature; Its Bearing on Theology and History of Religion* (Edinburgh: T. and T. Clark, 1936), p. 20.

[3] *Der Prediger* (Leipzig: D. Werner Scholl, 1932), p. 44.

But because of all this the writer is in even greater despair than Job—he no longer even expects God to "speak" and reveal himself. He has long since concluded that the rule of God, even if it be rational and moral, can never be grasped by men in its essential nature. God hides his purpose (7:13 f.); his sovereign acts are beyond understanding and beyond change, and man is utterly helpless before them.

In a comment upon the little piece of skepticism which introduces the Wisdom of Agur in the Book of Proverbs, C. H. Toy remarks that "whereas elsewhere in the Old Testament the greatness of God is treated as a ground for awe and reverence; here it is regarded as a reason for refraining from attempts to define him."[4] It seems that Toy should really have added Ecclesiastes to this exception. Unlike Job, its writer has ceased to try to understand God.

An awareness of man's frailty is no new thing in the Old Testament. Creaturehood, dependence, brevity of life—these are characteristic notes throughout; but elsewhere they are coupled with admonitions to live obediently and fruitfully in the time allotted. By learning wisdom, which is the way of God, the frail powers may be utilized to the full (Ps. 90:12). The eagerness for long life, everywhere emphasized, is itself an indication that the Israelite believed in the goodness of life and in the reward on earth that virtue brings. But in Job and Ecclesiastes this consciousness of frailty is, for the first time, coupled with a sense of tragedy and futility. They are no longer interested in long life.

For Job life is tragic because he is held responsible by a

[4] *The Book of Proverbs* (New York: Charles Scribner's Sons, 1908), p. xix.

moral God whom he can neither fathom nor discover. He recognizes that man is a driven leaf and dry stubble (13:25—14:2), and man reminds him of the fleeting shadow and of the desert blossom that fades so soon. Like a motheaten garment or a rotten thing, man's life falls apart; yet he is held to account. That is the tragedy that makes Job long for death. Man's life is unbearable because his way is "hid." God seems to ask more of man than he is legitimately entitled to demand, man being his own frail creature.

For Ecclesiastes life is just futile. The writer has almost ceased to worry about the brevity of life and about man's return to the dust whence he came. Man's frailty is epitomized by the cosmic ignorance to which he is forever doomed; for God has decreed that man shall not know his work (3:11–14; 6:10; 7:15, 24 f.). No one can explain the present; no one knows the future—man is helpless and life is futile.

The moral earnestness of Job is often contrasted with Ecclesiastes. Job feels that he is a sinner before God; and so are all men (7:21; 9:28 ff.). He wants to learn to know God's character so that he may know what his sins are. His sense of sinfulness is simply an implication of his faith that God is moral and holds men morally responsible.

Ecclesiastes, having decided that man's life can never be measured by the divine character, is not interested in sin against God as Job is. Since God cannot be known, how can he be obeyed? Ignorance of the law is an excuse! But Ecclesiastes does make a distinction between right and wrong in human relations; he reveals a sharp sense of justice (3:16; 4:1; 7:15; 8:10, 14). Ethically, he is a relativist, recognizing no absolute. His continued distinction in moral values on the purely human level, despite his inability to ground them in deity or in the cosmic order, must be related to his conception of the value of human wisdom. Job and Ecclesiastes do not really believe that man can find wisdom. Rather, the wisdom he can attain is of only relative value, since it is of no help in understanding God's moral rule of men. In the Job dialogue, Eliphaz declares that so often people of Job's stamp die without having obtained wisdom; but, for Eliphaz, wisdom seems to consist solely in an acknowledgment of man's sinfulness and in a corresponding explanation of trouble as discipline (4:17–21; 5:17 f.). He hints that Job's type is too eager to see the reason for things and to have empirical proof; such people are like the wicked in relying on their own power (5:12 ff.). God's purpose is so much greater than man's understanding of it that even the wise cannot grasp the nature of the divine righteousness as it applies to men (9:4 f.).

Job complains that his friends counsel him with the same ineffective knowledge that constitutes his own wisdom (26:3). What they offer him is only a palliative, and he knows it as well as they, for he has a mind like theirs (12:3). But it is the wisdom that man cannot discover and which God refrains from divulging that holds the "secret" of Job's problem (11:6). Seeing that Job refuses to put his faith in the disciplinary theory of trouble, which they call wisdom, the friends refer him to the lore which is the possession of the elders and the sages (8:8 ff.; 15:10). But to this, too, Job refuses to grant absolute value. The favorite proverb, "With the aged is wisdom; and length of days is understanding," he refutes with the declaration that wisdom and understanding are the prerogatives of deity (12:12 ff.). Job refuses to define pious faith as wisdom; he also rejects lore, which may have relative value for daily living but which fails to define empirically the ultimate moral ruler.

The Elihu section seems to be more ready to admit the divine initiative in the acquisition of wisdom. Wisdom, it says, is not just the gift of experience brought by the years; it is the gift of the divine spirit in man (32:8; 33:33). Because of God's special revelation to him, Elihu may counsel Job. The closing lines of the document seem to contrast those who seek for wisdom with their natural faculties with those who "fear" God (37:23 f.). In Elihu, as in Proverbs, chapters 1-9, there is an emphasis upon a special divine initiative, conditioned by man's humility, which supplements and assists independent natural inquiry; but this divine initiative is not yet connected with any specific way or object of special grace. We are on a line that balances the double emphasis upon faith and reason. Elihu's wisdom is his own, but it is a wisdom of faith rather than of reason.

For the writer of the dialogue proper, true wisdom is a divine secret. This is best illustrated in the passage which refers to the mythological *Urmensch* (15:7). This being appropriated the Divine Wisdom, which, apparently was preexistent (cf. Prov. 8:25).

The theme of the poem on Divine Wisdom included in the Book of Job (chap. 28) seems to be that man is wholly incapable of grasping the purposes of his creator, since true wisdom is unattainable. Man can discover rich treasures; he can mine the deep recesses of the earth for precious gems; but wisdom or the way to it he cannot find (28:12 ff., 20 ff.). In startling contrast, the Book of Proverbs tells us that gold and precious stones cannot be exchanged for it (Prov. 4:7; 8:11). Wisdom dwells neither on earth nor in She'ol; only God knows where it dwells. We are reminded of the apocalyptic Book of Enoch, which says that Wisdom had refused a dwelling place on earth. In search of such a place, it had found none where there was righteousness; so it had gone back to heaven whence it would return in messianic times (Enoch, chap. 44; 94:5; 5:8; 48:1; 49:1, 3). Ernest Sellin has described the poem as a "declaration of bankruptcy by a wisdom teacher"; yet there is some faith for the future.

The dwelling place of Divine Wisdom is very differently explained in the optimistic Wisdom Literature. In the Book of Proverbs Divine Wisdom is presented as living among men (8:12), where it blends naturally with human wisdom or prudence. This Wisdom, which takes up its station in the broad places and makes its home with "shrewd prudence," is the same Divine Wisdom participating in creation (8:22). We are not told here how it came to earth. Ben Sira tells us that this Wisdom was poured out upon all mankind, that it was created with the faithful in the womb, and that it also remained regnant with God in heaven (1:10, 14; 24: 3 ff.). Divine Wisdom found a resting place in Israel and ministered in the temple; all were invited to come and receive her and were offered full reward. Then Ben Sira equated the Divine Wisdom with the Law of Moses. In the Book of Baruch Divine Wisdom also dwelt in heaven; and men could not bring it to earth (3:29). But God gave it to Israel in the form of the Law. But in Job the Law and Divine Wisdom are not identified; there is no present gift of grace to give relief.

In Job the conviction that man cannot discover the way of life by the use of natural faculties alone is evoked by material reverses. The orthodox doctrine of rewards for the obedient has not justified itself. Presumably, if Job had only been prosperous, all would have been well, and he would have been content to rest in a terrestrial eschatology according to which God punishes sin and rewards virtue on earth. The fleeting and temporal character of God's plan for an individual which this eschatology implies seems not to have troubled the writer.

Émile Podechard has pointed out that this is hardly true in the case of Ecclesiastes.[5] The Preacher appears surfeited with all the goods that constitute "reward." It is true, of course, that he rebels at the injustices all around him, which seem to belie the orthodox doctrine; but what galls him most bitterly is man's brevity of life and his inability to control those who are to succeed him on earth. He is a defeatist because the doctrine is that the purposefulness of a man's life ends with the grave. For the Preacher, more than for Job, the earth has become too small and its best rewards too fleeting. In this sense and in this negative manner, he becomes, even more than Job, the harbinger of a belief in immortality. He himself utterly denies any purpose in existence beyond death (2:16–21; 5:14; 6:6; 9:5, 10); but his view of historical existence for man is so futile that some new view becomes imperative if life is to have significance.

The absolute, Divine Wisdom seems utterly unattainable to Ecclesiastes. God's activity and purpose, if such there be, cannot be uncovered. Human ingenuity even seems to have destroyed man's righteous nature as created by God (7:29).

[5] *L'Ecclésiaste* (Paris: Librairie Victor Le Coffre, 1912), pp. 196 f.

This seems to reflect the influence of Genesis in the Preacher: Man's desire to know produces the "Fall"; civilization is all a mistake. All man's thought and investigation have failed to bring him to a single focus that issues in a basic guide for action, while his effort simply increases worry and pain (1: 18; 2:18–23). Hertzberg describes the attitude in these words: "Der Strebende, das Erstrebte, das Streben selbst, alles nacheinander steht unter dem Fluch. Alles ist eitel: 'Ich sehe dass wir nichts wissen können.' "[6] Even practical, prudential rules seem unreliable. The multiplication of a wealth of empirical data and detail ends with a network of relationships that is confusing rather than enlightening. The wise cannot secure his future (2:19) and succumbs to temptation (7:7). Bread, riches, and reputation are the accidents of fate and birth, not the result of the work of the sages (9:11 f.). The man who begets a hundred children is no better off than a stillborn infant (2:14; 7:3 f., 8). Even every-day prudence is blighted because its results all come under the ultimate question, "What does it profit?" And the answer to that question is always the same: "Nothing."

Man's pragmatic wisdom has no ultimate value, which is one side of the picture; but it does have a relative and temporary value. Hence a man must remain active and play an ardent role in life (11:5 f.). It is true that one sinner is enough to upset all the efforts of prudential human planning; yet it is better to engage in such planning than to be a fool (2:13 f.; 4:13; 7:4 f.; 9:16–18; 10:2 ff.). Like the writers of the Book of Proverbs, he makes a sharp distinction between the wise and the fools. Fools are an inferior

6 *Op. cit.*, p. 81.

class of people, silly, loud, and noisy; they lack self-control, poise, and graciousness (5:3; 7:6, 9, 17; 10:12 ff.); they are not gentlemen. Besides, their indifferent attitude makes it impossible for them to understand man's true situation in life, unattractive as that may be.

The Preacher is a wise man. The lore of the sages, to which he denies ultimate significance, is the instrument he uses to inquire into the nature of life. Even his pessimistic conclusions cannot gainsay the fact that he was able, by means of human insight, to attain them (1:13). This profit, at least, his wisdom brings.

So all his conclusions about the worthlessness of human wisdom must be qualified. This human wisdom, limited but real in value, can best be described as knowledge that comes by reason (Fr. *science*). It is human intelligence in action and is superior to brute force (2:13 f.; 9:13, 16); but its advantages end with life on earth. The real rule by which God governs men, if there be such a rule, is never unveiled by this human wisdom. It is "humanistic" in a stricter sense than the wisdom in the oldest strata of the Book of Proverbs, because in no sense does the divine mind come to consciousness in it; but it does enable its possessor to harden himself manfully against inevitable fate and confirm his self-control. His code for living has been summed up as follows: "Death is better than life; grief is more becoming than mirth; contemplation is preferable to desire; and deliberation is more serviceable than haste."[7]

The wisdom discounted in Job and Ecclesiastes is the same as the wisdom in the oldest sections of Proverbs—it

[7] E. J. Dillon, *The Skeptics of the Old Testament: Job, Koheleth, Agur* (London: Isbister & Co., Ltd., 1895), pp. 10 f.

is natural human wisdom. Human reason, empirical observation through the use of all faculties, and objective judgment mark its process of development in man. It consists of the accumulated lore of the centuries placed at the disposal of free and alert minds that share their findings, and gray-haired experience is its hallmark. Job and Ecclesiastes conclude that it is the only sort of wisdom available to man, while Proverbs senses no need for any other sort. It is to be attained by means of natural endowments of man, not by a supernatural initiative supplementing creation.

The only difference is that Proverbs expected more of this human wisdom. To Job and Ecclesiastes the results are much less satisfying. Why? In the wisdom movement they disposed of a more mature insight. There was a more detailed and discriminating analysis of what the results really amounted to; also, like every other human movement as it proceeds on its way, youthful ardor and faith had been tempered—there were failures to point to in past experience as well as successes. The movement had turned from action to speculation; instead of experimenting with new ways for living and with new rules for life, it deplored the fact that the present rules did not suffice and entered upon metaphysical explanations to account for it.

In earlier wisdom documents human wisdom began with God in the sense that all man's natural endowments and the world in which he puts them to work are God's creation; this is also true in Job and Ecclesiastes. Man's wisdom is human in the sense that only human processes are employed in its acquisition. However, those who seek wisdom do not think that it is an isolated human phenomenon, because there is no doubt about an all-comprehensive existing intelligence. "With him are wisdom and power; he has counsel and understanding" (Job 12:13). The problem man faces is how he may grasp more of that intelligence. The conviction grows in the pessimistic wisdom writings that the measure of human intelligence is too limited. How can man grasp the Divine Wisdom? The gap between it and human wisdom has become much wider than it was in the Book of Proverbs.

A contrast between the wisdom of God as creator and of man as creature had always been recognized. That contrast now seems sharper because of man's apparent inability to know God as he should know him to obey him and so win his favor. This raises a crucial question: Are human and Divine Wisdom mutually exclusive? In the early strata of Proverbs that question turned about the problem of the religious interest of natural human wisdom. Here it may be said to turn about its capacity for religion. The interest is clearly enough displayed. Does this human wisdom arrive at any true understanding of God? Is the wisdom so fearlessly used by Job and Ecclesiastes to estimate the human situation different in kind or in degree from the Divine Wisdom? Is it false, religiously speaking? Or is it merely incomplete?

It is as religion and theology that the human wisdom shows itself most frequently in the books of Job and Ecclesiastes. One must thus be prepared to take an utterly irrationalistic, "Barthian," position and maintain that its religious speculation is wholly at variance with truth and to deny its relatedness to the Divine Wisdom which resides only in heaven. In view of the role which these documents play in the historical development of Jewish religion, it would be very difficult to deny the relation between human and Divine Wisdom. To state that the use of human wisdom in them did not contribute to the revelation of religious truth is to challenge the validity of many of the doctrines developed in later Judaism and in Christianity, especially a supra-historical eschatology. It is the critical work of Job and Ecclesiastes upon the earlier orthodox position that lays the groundwork for these later developments.

These documents represent a last-stand effort to hold the wisdom movement to the rationalistic and natural methods with which it began. Because of the increasing pressure of the transcendentalism in the national religious tradition and because of the movement's own increasingly speculative interest, this effort did not win the day. Its contribution to the Jewish religious system was not so much to emphasize the necessity for some form of belief in divine initiative in revelation, since Jewish religion in its main stream had always had that; the real function of these documents is a critical one—they help to clear the ground for new growth.

The real contribution of Job and Ecclesiastes was to help to smash the too limited, earth-bound arena of traditional Jewish eschatology, which the great prophetic movement had utterly failed to do. By their rigid analysis and merciless criticism of life in the light of the orthodox doctrine of rewards, the pessimistic writers paved the way for a new eschatology, in which the rewards of religion were more in keeping with a religion that made moral and spiritual demands. In it, too, the eschatological arena was more commensurate with the realm of the purposes of the universal and eternal God, to whom Judaism looked and in whose image it believed man to be created. This implied the introduction of a doctrine of immortality or resurrection. In making this contribution the empirical and rationalistic wisdom movement sealed its own demise.

We have noted that in the early Wisdom Literature the introduction of the Divine Wisdom to the human came about most naturally—natural and revealed religion were indistinguishable, as it were; there was no gap between nature and grace. The divine initiative did not limit itself to a peculiar instrumentality or tradition that made it more accessible to some than to others. It addresses itself directly to people, regardless of their nation and without intermediaries. All this is best illustrated in Proverbs, chapters 1-9. It also seems to be true in the Elihu document (32:8).

This situation ceases as soon as the nationalization of wisdom is accomplished. God's initiative henceforth is not accessible to all; it has lost its universal appeal. Wisdom is now predominantly God's gift to men rather than man's own discovery. The strong emphasis upon the divine initiative destroys the earlier synergistic harmony. Grace—the gift aspect—is increasingly added to nature until it finally plays the dominant role; and the limits of grace are no longer coterminous with natural discovery, since it is identified so closely with localized embodiments, of which the Law is most conspicuous. Men can be saved only by grace.

Even with this ascendancy of grace, nature is not wholly annihilated, because it is not an enemy of grace. Its methods —travel, observation of natural phenomena and of human behavior, reason, and forum discussion—are now all subservient to the divine, God's gift of grace to Israel. Yet these avenues of social discovery are blended with this grace; they provide the latter with something to work on—a foundation, as it were.

The Wisdom of Solomon, Baruch, and IV Maccabees are even more thorough in their conception of grace than Ben Sira. The all-permeating activity of the Divine Wisdom and human helplessness without the Law are their cardinal doctrines to witness to this (Wisd. of Sol. 8:7; Bar. 4:1; IV Macc. 5:16–20). Yet the honorable place given to the standard Greek virtues in two of these books seems to indicate that the results of the human search for wisdom, even in paganism, were felt as helping to clear the way for this grace, which, for them, is man's true hope. There is no denial of the relatedness of divine and human rationality.

It seems a legitimate inference that these "means of grace" were being introduced and emphasized as a reaction to the feeling of despair that had overcome the rationalistic wisdom seekers, such as Job and Ecclesiastes. Ben Sira is probably a response to the latter; the Wisdom of Solomon quite evidently is. While the swing of the pendulum toward "irrationalism" was strong, the line between the two focuses, nature and grace, does not seem to have broken.

The creation of such intermediary agencies as the Divine Word, the Law, the Spirit, and the Divine Wisdom is in itself an argument for the harmony that continued to exist between human and divine knowledge. It is difficult to define these agencies precisely; there is, for example, no agreement on when such an intermediary may be described as a hypostasis; but, whatever the definition, their express function is to serve as a bridge to span the gap between heaven and earth.

By becoming an intermediary, the Divine Wisdom is no longer only in heaven but also on earth. Thus it makes common effort with the human intelligence, which is able to apprehend it in its self-giving capacity. Speaking of this, Wilhelm Schencke says: "Man muss also *a priori* erwarten, entweder dass die himmliche Weisheit doch nach der Erde hinunter gebracht wird, oder dass eine Verknüpfung zwischen der göttlichen und der menschlichen Weisheit statt findet."[8] Even if it came to earth in the form of a rigid external code which claimed to report the truth about God's character, it gave the human mind something to work on and to relate its own discoveries to. This was even more true when it came in more personal and experiential ways as Spirit or Word.

By means of these divine aids, usually too severely bound by a particularistic tradition, the human search could be continued. The initial freedom of this search was lost; but the despair that its rationalism had produced was also overcome. The aids were evoked in an era of despair in the natural wisdom movement; but they were possible because that movement was basically always convinced that man is a part of a created order. Faith is restored by means of special gifts, whose source is the same as the source of man's natural endowments. Faith has a new method of vindicating itself.

Faith is the conviction that right triumphs. In the early period of the movement this was believed to be empirically demonstrable. The results produced on earth for those who adhered to belief in a moral and just God and who lived

---

[8] Schencke, *Die Chokma (Sophia) in der jüdischen Hypostosenspekulation* (Kristiana: A. W. Brøggers, 1913), p. 27.

accordingly would be the empirical justification of faith. The corollaries of probation and discipline in the doctrine of rewards did not basically alter this view. Job and Ecclesiastes did not give up the conviction that God was moral or that right triumphs; but they did doubt that it was possible to verify this empirically by a demonstration of results. They were despondent because they found it impossible to surrender this opportunity of testing for themselves both the rule that governed them and the results that showed its sovereignty.

The new confidence and the optimistic faith in the later wisdom writings are made possible by a surrender of this doctrine of empirical verification so dear to the earlier, more naturalistic wisdom writers. The new faith relies entirely upon the Law as its guide for conduct and considers the Law an unerring expression of the Divine Wisdom by which man must be guided. Though this Law is actually in large measure the result of social experience and discovery in the past, it is now to be accepted uncritically. Since it is the product of an earlier day, it can no longer be tested in any free, contemporary inquiry based on an empirical observation of life—it is authoritarian. Even though, as in Ben Sira, the rewards are still expected on earth, the arena in which they are given is no longer the arena in which the demands are discovered. If, as in the other later wisdom material, they are granted in the beyond, they obviously lie beyond empirical verification as well.

In the Book of Job the argument turns about the validity of the old faith, according to which the rewards must be empirically demonstrable. The friends defend it; Job questions it. The intimations of immortality and a future vindication of the righteous, however seriously taken, fail to give Job that justification for his faith which he seeks (14:14; 19:25 f.). These would only restore his faith at the price of the very verification he seeks.

The concluding poem in Job celebrates the transcendence of God and the consequent inscrutability of his ways (38:1 —41:34). Its aim seems to be to show that the desire to understand the ways of God was presumptuous. Some interpreters see in this poem an effort to eliminate reward entirely as an element in religious motivation and put it on a plane with Psalm 73 and Habakkuk. Whatever merit this view may have, it is clear that faith is asked to stand without benefit of demonstration either of the rule it follows or of the results it expects. It forms another chapter in the reorientation of wisdom.

Ben Sira was probably aware of the analysis of the human situation made by Job and Ecclesiastes; but he refused to accept their gloomy interpretation of the scene. He is not ready to admit that the accepted rules of life do not work out; and the certainty of death does not produce in him the ennui it did for Ecclesiastes (Ben Sira 14:18–20). He has more confidence in the generations yet to come; he trusts that they will diligently use the results of his toil. Whatever memorial they feel his name justifies will be sufficient reward for him. Thus his eschatology is still wholly historical. Allowing for the corollaries to the doctrine of rewards, the results of obedience to the Law can still be verified. But the basis of his faith—the Law which is the rule of the wisdom by which the rewards must come—is no longer open to full criticism; contemporary social discovery must be modified to fit it.

The Book of Baruch must be understood along the same lines; for it emphasizes even more severely the divine, transcendent character of the Law and offers less historical basis for the conviction that the nation is heir of a divine election. The Law has become man's master rather than the instrument of his own discovery. Both in Ben Sira and in Baruch this rule of wisdom becomes an item in the faith which man has in God's moral governance rather than a reasoned basis for it. It cannot be critically dealt with because it is supposed to be a special gift that transcends all man's native endowments. The rule that leads to wisdom now is grace received by faith rather than the human basis for faith, as was the case in the earlier stages of the wisdom movement. Man's wisdom has become transcendental, and the emergence of a transcendental eschatology is now only a matter of time.

We have already seen that in the Wisdom of Solomon and IV Maccabees immortality and future judgment become the real reward for obedience to the transcendent Law. Ben Sira almost unwittingly, Baruch most explicitly, and these later documents quite joyfully make that surrender of human reason over which Job had agonized. In IV Maccabees the usual term—δ $\epsilon\dot{v}\sigma\epsilon\beta\acute{\eta}s$ $\lambda o\gamma\iota\sigma\mu\acute{o}s$—is exchanged three times over for the genitive construction—δ $\lambda o\gamma\iota\sigma\mu\acute{o}s$ $\tau\hat{\eta}s$ $\epsilon\dot{v}\sigma\epsilon\beta\epsilon\iota as$ (7:4, 24; 16:4). This seems to indicate that in the co-operation of natural and Divine Wisdom the latter was in control. It was not the writer's intent to inculcate a sort of reverent rationalism comparable to the earliest sections of Proverbs. Concepts of causability, origin, and possession are implied in these genitives. Piety, it seems, played the chief role in the writer's mind; and this piety consisted in acceptance of, and obedience to the divine Law. He stood for reason enabled and controlled by faith. The relationship reminds André Dupont-Sommer of the Scholastic attitude:

Dans cette alliage, c'est même la piété qui l'emporte. Pour définir les relations entre la raison et la foi, les Scolastiques hésitaient entre deux formules: *intellectus quaerens fidem* ou *fides quaerens intellectum*. On peut hésiter aussi à propos de notre auteur. Nulle frontière précise ne sépare en lui le domaine de la croyance et celui de la speculation, et sa pensée se meut de l'un à l'autre sans obstacle, sans heurt, sans effort; mais au fond de son âme la foi regne sans contestes, et la raison lui est entièrement soumise, *ancilla theologiae*.[9]

Full criticism of the way to God and full verification of the rewards are now alike precluded. Men now live by a transcendent faith, and they do so eagerly, heroically, and loyally. Though this faith gave reason second place, it was not wholly irrational; there was not a complete cessation of human initiative or of empirical verification, any more than there is in classical Catholicism.

The synergism is well illustrated in the Wisdom of Solomon. There the Divine Wisdom is an unlimited divine potency, permeating all existence (7:22—8:1); but it is also a special gift to men that enables them to rule wisely, to love God, and to attain immortality (9:13–18; 7:14; 6:2; 8:13, 17). This Divine Wisdom comes to men from beside the throne of God; but, as a human possession, it operates in man by and through human faculties. Thus there is a close *Verknüpfung* between natural gifts and gifts of grace.

[9] *Le Quatrième Livre des Machabées; Introduction, Traduction, et Notes* (Paris: Libraire Ancienne Honoré Champion, 1939), p. 36.

Moreover, this wisdom is self-attained; before men can receive it, they must be morally worthy of it (6:9; 7:27), they must seek it in prayer (9:18). This gift of grace is not irresistible. So, even in the acquisition of Divine Wisdom as a special gift, human initiative continued to play its role. The ever present tension of natural human freedom and a sovereign divine rule are held in balance in this synergistic pattern. Both man and God contribute to the acquisition of Divine Wisdom. The balance has shifted sharply toward the divine dominance since we first observed the tension in the Hebrew wisdom movement. Nevertheless, specific, empirically discernible rewards continue to be planned for and to be earned, which came to characterize the difference between the Law-wisdom movement and the apocalyptic movement, which scorned human reason and earthly values much more completely. Human efforts and material rewards now played a secondary role in the wisdom movement. In times of frustration, stress, and trial men rested on divine gifts and eternal hopes. Wisdom was now transcendent. Men had it as a gift.

We have thus far attempted to understand the historical development and meaning of the concept of wisdom by treating it as an index to the ideas about revelation that were current in the wisdom circles. Even the general oriental background of the Hebrew wisdom movement displayed an alternating optimism and despair about the natural human capacity for wisdom. Like the early Hebrew movement, it recognized that all natural human capacities are the divine endowment of a created order of which man is a part and that limitations of natural capacities provide a place for faith in a divine initiative and grace beyond nature. We have attempted to show that in the Hebrew wisdom movement there is evidence of a continuous tension and, by the same token, of an unbroken continuity between reason and grace, nature and supernature, discovery and revelation. This continuity is rooted in man's simultaneous awareness of creaturehood and freedom.

Nowhere in the Old Testament tradition has human freedom such a natural and independent course as in the early stages of the wisdom movement. Nowhere has divine transcendence greater emphasis than in the later stages of the same movement. The results produced by an emphasis upon either extreme contribute to its opposite: the extreme rationalism of Job and Ecclesiastes ushered in a new eschatology, more transcendent than anything Hebrew religion had ever known. The tension did not snap; for there was always an overlapping of nature and grace. This should be remembered by all who seek to understand the meaning of revelation in the later developments of the Hebrew-Christian tradition. The tension so long maintained and so basic in the roots of Jewish-Christian religious development cannot be ignored by those who would formulate a theology today.

It remains to compare the wisdom concept with that of spirit; for spirit, with wisdom, is a common index to Hebrew ideas about revelation. We must see how the interrelationships and identification of functions that developed between these two finally affected those ideas about revelation for which wisdom was the index; that is, how the Spirit changed Wisdom's role in revelation.

CHAPTER V

WISDOM AND THE SPIRIT

UP TO now we have traced the development of the Hebrew wisdom movement from its international beginnings to its absorption by the national religious tradition, and we have seen the effect that this has had upon the tradition itself. We have sought to understand the various meanings of the concept of wisdom by treating it as an index to the ideas of revelation held by those who employed it. The meaning attached to the term at various times and by different groups was indicative of the way in which they thought that they obtained knowledge of God and of his rule over men.

In this final chapter we wish to analyze further the wisdom concept as an instrument of revelation and knowledge by comparing it with the Old Testament concept of spirit. The ideas held about the latter can also be used as an index to the ideas about revelation that prevailed in the religion of Israel. We must note the interrelationships of function that are achieved between these two concepts, whose initial beginnings are so very different. And we must note how, in its sharing the same functions as spirit, the wisdom concept itself was changed.

Spirit, like Word, Law, and Wisdom, is treated as an independent agency in the later Jewish period, although for our purpose it is not necessary to attempt to determine the degree of this independence, since the whole question of hypostatization is an intricate one about which no agreement exists. Besides, it would be impossible to attempt a definition of the precise status of these agencies in Judaism without a detailed analysis of their development in the New Testament and in patristic literature. That is not within our compass; we are interested simply in the functional comparison of Wisdom and Spirit.

Just as we found that Wisdom was frequently equated with the Law, so we now note that it is likewise equated with Spirit (Exod. 28:3; 31:3; 35:1; Deut. 34:9; Job 32:8; Wisd. of Sol. 1:7; 9:17; 11:20). Spirit is also equated with the concept of word (Pss. 33:6, 9; 104:30; 147:18; Ezek. 11:5; Mic. 3:8; Jth. 16:14; II Bar. 21:4). But we note that there is apparently no equation of the Spirit with the Law.

The basic idea in the word "wisdom," whether it be related to man or to God, is always "intelligence." Similarly, the most original and central idea in the word "spirit," whether it is met in nature, man, or God, is "power or energy." Such other aspects as morality and intelligence in the concept of "spirit" are best described as assimilations attending the development of that basic idea. In the beginning, spirit seems to have been impersonal force.

The Hebrew word for "spirit" is *ruaḥ;* its Greek equivalent is *pneuma*. It is the word for "wind" (Gen. 8:1; Exod. 10:13, 19), and it also connotes "human breath" (Gen. 7:22; Ps. 150:6). It is the term that describes the principle of human life, *psyche* (Num. 27:16; Pss. 31:6; 77:4). It is used to describe emotional states, such as confidence and fear, the reactions of a human personality to a situation (Gen. 45:27; Num. 5:14, 30; Isa. 61:3). It may refer to a man's intelligent, purposive faculties, to his mind (Pss. 32:2; 78:8; Prov. 1:23; Dan. 2:3), and in one instance the word refers to what is best described as a man's conscience (Mal. 2:15 f.). In all these uses spirit is an integral part of human life, a permanent possession of man. It is true that this natural endowment is frequently described as a divine gift. But it is a gift in the order of creation, not a special gift. Of that we shall speak later.

It is quite understandable how the same term was used to describe the wind, human breath, and physical life-energy. By refinement, emotional, intellectual, and moral aspects were distinguished in this human energy; so likewise, thinking objectively, men associated the wind with the whole cosmic energy by which they felt their lives to be controlled and determined.

Some students of the history of the growth of religious ideas are of the opinion that, preceding all ideas of personal deity, men lived under the impression that there was an all-pervasive, energizing, noumenal force. In Hebrew this would be designated by the word *ruaḥ*. The natural wind was a phenomenon produced by it; and man's possession of breath and energy made him feel related to this cosmic power.

According to this theory, a growing differentiation in this impersonal force produced localizations and personalizations that led to animism (with demonism) and then to polytheism. For a long time, it is held, the impersonal *ruaḥ* was the more comprehensive power to which the developing gods were subordinate. There is an opposite school of thought, chiefly Catholic, which contends that from the very beginning *ruaḥ* was thought of as the breath of a personal deity to whom it was subordinate.[1] Whatever the nature of this early development, it antedates the Old Testament record. But the irrational, dynamic, and nonmoral character of what are declared to be manifestations of the Divine Spirit are still clearly evident in the Old Testament, whatever the antecedents that made it so.

In the Old Testament as we now have it this divine *ruaḥ* is always described as a possession of deity and subordinate to it. Its turbulent, dynamic character is well illustrated where the deeds of Yahweh are compared to those of a storm-god. The wind becomes "the fierce breath of his anger" or "the blast of his nostrils" (II Sam. 22:16; Exod. 15:8; Isa. 11:15; 59:15). In later refinements the winds become "messengers" of Yahweh. Gradually, as the whole concept of deity is moralized, these expressions relating to its power serve his moral purposes; but power and energy continue as the basic ideas of the spirit concept (Isa. 59:19; cf. also Isa. 11:9, which refers to the Messiah).

In later sections of the Old Testament the dynamic operation of spirit in God is bounded by his moral and intelligent qualities. The Spirit is now described as holy (Ps. 51:11). God himself is described as a spirit of justice for those who will enjoy justice in the future age (Isa. 28:6). The designs of God are even said to originate in his spirit (Isa. 40:13). Thus gradually spirit begins to constitute the mind of God as well as his moral character. Wisdom, understanding, counsel, knowledge, the fear of the Lord, power, justice, strength, and judgment are the attributes of this spirit of God (Isa. 4:4; Mic. 3:8; Isa. 11:2 f.). Thus we see how, in

[1] Paul van Imschoot, "L'Esprit de Jahvé: principe de vie morale," *Ephemerides theologiae Louvainensis*, XVI (1939), 459.

the integration of the Hebrew concept of deity, wisdom and spirit, two elements in it that begin at opposite poles, are gradually drawn together and begin to operate in the same orbit. Spirit and Wisdom acquire identical functions in the creation of the world and in its moral governance. In creation the Spirit appears as a cosmic principle. In Genesis it broods upon the face of the waters at the time of God's creative activity. In Judith the personified spirit is the agency by which God formed all things (16:14). The heavens and all living creatures are made by the breath of the mouth of God; that breath keeps the creatures in life; when it is removed they perish (Job 34:14; Pss. 33:6; 104:30). The role is analogous to that played by Wisdom as God's instrument in creation (Prov. 8:22–31; Ben Sira 24:3–5; Wisd. of Sol. 7:22; 8:1).

Both Wisdom and the Spirit sustain creation and govern it morally; and Spirit is capable of the wisdom of purpose and design. As a moral power the Divine Spirit is everywhere; it brings judgment and destruction upon the nations that have transgressed. It even penetrates to She'ol (Isa. 11:15; 30:28; 34:16; Ps. 139:7; Ezek. 10:17). In the Wisdom of Solomon the identification of these two agencies becomes explicit and conscious. The Spirit of the Lord fills the whole inhabited world and holds all things together. It has complete knowledge of all human thought and speech, passing judgment upon it. This Wisdom-Spirit, which is all-penetrating and omniscient, is the "breath of the power of God" (1:6; 7:24).

In these identical functions of creation and moral governance the equation of Wisdom with Spirit is established.

Spirit began as the power quality of a tribal deity; now it plays a role in the cosmic and moral governance of the creation. This role corresponds to Yahweh's development as the universal ruler. The manifestations of the Divine Spirit among men, at first intensely nationalistic, now transcend the tribal limitations and approach the internationalism that was typical of Wisdom.

Both Wisdom and Spirit have been described as natural human possessions and as integral attributes of God. There is still a further similarity between the two. Like Wisdom, the Divine Spirit is frequently imparted to men as a special gift from deity, transcending natural creaturely endowments. It may, like Wisdom, be a gift of grace.

The earliest of these special gifts of Spirit to men make them excel in physical power (Judg. 3:10; 11:29; 13:25; Isa. 10:6 ff.; 16:13). This agrees with the basic concept of the Spirit as energy—the gifts being elements of physical daring, passion, and brute strength. One detects no particular moral differentiation. By virtue of the gift of Spirit there is aroused a violent clan or tribal loyalty; and this aroused tribal consciousness is coupled with a strict performance of cultic rites as illustrated by Samson's Nazirite vow and Saul's contacts with the seer Samuel (Judg. 13:3-5; I Sam. 9:23—10:1). It seems quite legitimate to draw a close analogy between the tribal war dances of the American Indians or of the African tribes today and the ecstatic revelry of the *n'bi'im*, among whom Saul was seized by the Spirit. Music, rhythmic dancing by the group, and occasional possession play their role. The special gifts of Spirit produced ardor in the devotees of a tribal cult.

It is pertinent to observe that these special gifts of the

Spirit were often very temporary and given to carry out specific functions. Furthermore, they were much more immediately related to situations in human experience than was the case with Wisdom as a special gift. This is particularly true where the special divine gift of Wisdom is identified with the Mosaic Law, which was so frequently the case.

There are also special gifts of evil spirit, which are described as coming from Yahweh. In those receiving such gifts, they replace courage and daring with neuroticism (I Sam. 18:10; 19:10; I Kings 22:23), or, in the case of prophets, they give false messages. These manifestations of evil spirits may represent primitive demonic forces that biblical editors have brought under the control of Yahweh. They lack every trace of moral distinction. They are apparently irrational and are specific instances of "divine infatuation."

Spirit as a special gift of God to men also performed more elevated intellectual and moral functions, and, as such, it supplemented the natural human endowments of *ruaḥ*, already mentioned. At times the natural mind or spirit seems capable of an insight or a right moral choice on a par with that granted by the special gift of Spirit: It was the natural human spirit that prompted men to bring gifts for the tabernacle of Moses (Exod. 35:21); Caleb's own natural spirit seems to have made him trust Yahweh's plans (Num. 14: 24); Joshua's natural spirit qualified him to be chosen as a judge, although Moses laid hands on him to impart a special allotment of Divine Spirit which was needed in the actual execution of the office (Num. 27:18). It is noteworthy that Deut. 34:9, referring to the same incident, attributes Joshua's equipment entirely to the Divine Spirit.

The account of Joshua in Numbers strikingly illustrates the continuity of natural human action and divine action in the realm of spirit. In the famous penitential psalm the human spirit, broken before God, becomes the basis and condition on which the divine favor depends (51:19 [17]), which is, of course, that a human spirit that is not contrite and penitent is wicked. Natural human sinfulness is acknowledged; but, more significantly for our purpose, it implies an element of human freedom in the receipt of grace in the form of Spirit. God's special gift comes only to those who are morally ready for it and desirous of having it. As we saw earlier, such freedom is also maintained by men in the reception of Divine Wisdom as a special gift of grace (Wisd. of Sol. 1:4 f.; Isa. 63:10; cf. also Eph. 4:30).

Synergistic examples of human and Divine Spirit occur elsewhere. In the Apocrypha we are told that Daniel had a holy spirit (Sus., chap. 45). Perhaps this should not be taken in a natural sense, since all prophets had special allotments of Divine Spirit, according to the later centuries. But in Ezekiel men are told to get new spirits for themselves, or they are told that God will give them a new spirit (11:19; 18:31). Sometimes the human spirit is pictured as moved by God in some unspecified way to do his bidding (Ezek. 1:1; Hag. 1:14). In the Book of Jubilees a prayer placed in the mouth of Moses asks God to create in men a Holy Spirit to replace the spirit of Belial, which they now have (1:20). This is the language of a later age and hardly contemplates the extinction of the natural human spirit.

Nowhere do we find real evidence to indicate that the writers felt that the reception of Divine Spirit as a special gift meant the extinction of the natural human spirit. On the contrary, all evidence leads one to conclude that such special gifts, however indispensable, transformed or strengthened the efforts of the wicked or faltering human spirit in its moral purposes and decisions (Ps. 51:12). For this very reason it is often nearly impossible to distinguish between the human spirit simply as a natural creaturely endowment and those cases in which we are dealing with the Divine Spirit as a special gift of grace to men. Besides, it must be emphasized again that, even where the special gift of grace does not appear, divine influence is not utterly lacking; for with Spirit, as in the case of Wisdom, divine influence also operates through creation.

An interesting function of the Divine Spirit as a peculiar human possession enables specially designated individuals to execute properly the furnishing of the tent of assembly. The sons of Aaron and Bezalel receive this skill-imparting Spirit (Exod. 28:3; 31:3; 35:31). It is described both as the Spirit of God and as the Spirit of wisdom. In a sense its role is comparable to the Divine Wisdom because for the writer of wisdom this also became the principle of all scientific investigation and interpretation. Only here the Spirit's role as a guide in crafts and sciences seems limited exclusively to the sacred building and its objects. There was an aura of great awe and mystery about the shrine; it must, therefore, have seemed reasonable that only people specially enlightened could have constructed it. David's blueprint for the temple, given to Solomon, is likewise said to be a special revelation "by the spirit" (I Chron. 28:12).

Divine Spirit uniquely given to men was thus an instrument of special enlightenment and revelation. Those who possessed it were a class that understood God's way to an uncommon degree and were able to declare its demands. These men of the Spirit became the medium for divine oracles (Hos. 9:7) and were held capable of deeds that transcend human experience (II Kings 2:15). Their possession of the transcendent gift of the Spirit makes their behavior seem irrational to outsiders (I Kings 18:12). At times the natural human mind and spirit seem wholly lost in the divine gift and in no way in control of it, as, for example, the Divine Spirit, we are told, put on and used as a garment the human forms of Gideon, Amasai, and Zechariah (Judg. 6:34; I Chron. 12:18; II Chron. 24:20); thus the human individuals seem entirely a voice for the divine power. Often the Divine Spirit possesses an individual only for those moments in which the divine oracle is imparted (Num. 24:2; Isa. 19:20–24; I Kings 22:24).

Sometimes the Divine Spirit operates in behalf of people without making use of them in any form. In Haggai the Spirit comes to the nation's aid without being incarnate in any personality and seems to be synonymous with the pillar of fire that guided the nation in the Exodus (Hag. 2:5; cf. also Zech. 4:6). In the Wisdom of Solomon the Divine Wisdom is actually given this role of the pillar of fire (10:17).

What does this overpowering nature of the Divine Spirit do to the synergism between human and divine activity noted earlier? There is almost unanimous agreement that the earlier n^ebi'im were ecstatics, that is, they received their oracles while in a trance that made their natural intelligence momentarily inoperative, and when they recovered from their trance, they reported what they had seen or heard. The story of Mohammed presents a close parallel; and his followers use the assumed cessation of his natural intelligence during the revelation of the Koran as incontestible proof of its divine character.

Antonin Causse insists that, even where the oracle is received in this ecstatic experience that blots out natural faculties, it will not do to describe the recipients as pathological, as Lods has done.[2] To do so, he says, would fail to take account of the heightened powers of personality that are unmistakably produced in the characters who are the subjects of these ecstatic experiences One wonders if the assertion that personalities were strengthened by these experiences can be maintained for the n'bi'im? Over against the apparently positive development of character in men like Elijah and Elisha, one should perhaps weigh the quite evident signs of deterioration of personality in a man like Saul. Since he was also "among the prophets," his story may be indicative of others in this class of ecstatics. The story of Mohammed again offers an interesting analogy.

Causse and others who emphasize the ecstatic element in prophecy usually agree that this characteristic was less prominent among the writing prophets, and they acknowledge that the natural intelligence was active in the reception of the messages, at least to some extent. Besides, with the possible exception of Ezekiel, these pre-Exilic writing prophets do not themselves credit the Divine Spirit as the instrument by which their oracles are given.

It is as the instrument of divine revelation in early, ecstatic prophecy that the Divine Spirit, by its overpowering transcendence, comes nearest to wiping out the continuity

[2] "Quelques remarques sur la psychologie des prophètes," *Revue d'histoire et de philosophie religieuse*, II (1922), 349-56; cf. Adolph Lods, "Recherches sur le prophétisme israélite," *Revue de l'histoire des religions*, CIII-CIV (1931), 279-316.

between human and divine activity. Elsewhere this continuity is maintained in the roles both of Wisdom and of Spirit. It is clear what this break in continuity entails. If the role of human initiative was actually completely obliterated in the process by which they were given knowledge of the way of God, this would constitute the virtual and effective suppression of human personality. The natural, created order would have been annihilated by the special order of grace. Human freedom and personality are both denied at that point at which their significance would have been real. However this may be in the case of the n'bi'im, it certainly cannot be said to have happened in the later developments in which the Divine Spirit is featured as the principle of revelation and as the special divine gift to men.

The pre-Exilic writing prophets do not discuss the Divine Spirit. But elsewhere we receive the impression that there was a general conviction that these men possessed a special gift of the Spirit as a permanent possession and consciously under their control (Num. 11:26, 29; II Sam. 23:2; Hos. 9:7; Joel 3:1; Mic. 3:8; Wisd. of Sol. 7:27). This view must probably be attributed to a later era. The writers that record it exalt the personalities of the prophets as such, but they also emphasize the transcendence of the Divine Spirit who "spoke through them." As they see it, the Divine Spirit seems to have a curious double role, comparable to the role of the Law in the later Wisdom Literature. In one sense it is a divine agency or activity which uses men as its instruments; in another sense it is, by grace, a human possession and a human instrument used to ascertain the divine will.

In the former sense it tends to suppress natural human personality; in the latter it tends to exalt it. Like the Law, the Spirit can never be comprehended or controlled; yet, like the former, it must be interpreted and obeyed. The chief difference is that in both instances it operates within individuals, through experience.

Tosefta 13:2 shows that in some circles, especially the rabbinic, prophets were held to be the only possessors of the Spirit: "When the last prophets, Haggai, Zechariah, and Malachi, died, the Holy Spirit ceased out of Israel." The later prophets, beginning with Ezekiel, had again attributed their gift of prophecy to the Spirit (Ezek. 11:5; Isa. 48:16; 61:1; Zech. 7:12; Dan. 4:8).

While the rabbinic circle tended to limit the Spirit to the prophets, there are other indications that in the later era it was acquiring a wider place in the religious life of the nation. It was coming to be viewed as an abiding presence of enlightenment and encouragement—a gift to the entire nation. The Spirit is the assurance of God's personal presence to encourage the returned exiles in the rebuilding of the Temple. In the famous Servant Songs in the Book of Isaiah the servant possesses the Spirit. Lack of agreement on the identity of the servant, a subject of perennial dispute, makes it impossible to assign this gift of the Divine Spirit to the community. But, despite the present tendency to identify the servant as an individual, the possibility still remains.

Uncertainty of authorship attends the apparent assignment of the Spirit to the community in Isa. 59:21. Paul Volz feels that the writer of the document could not have made such an assignment and that this verse is a later addition or a misplaced fragment of the prophet's own words.[3] The latter alternative would eliminate the communal application. In view of the reference to the presence of the Spirit in future generations, this seems rather improbable. Both for individuals and for the community, the Divine Spirit becomes a gift which is used by men as an instrument of general moral and spiritual illumination (Ps. 143:10; Isa. 44:3). At the same time, that same Divine Spirit remains an independent principle of revelation and illumination, using men as its instruments or acting without any instrumental medium whatsoever.

We have already noted a similarity of functions for Wisdom and the Spirit. Both are cosmic principles playing similar roles in the creation of the world; both become special divine gifts to men, enabling them to know the divine purpose, which must be understood to such an extent that man's own life will have meaning and direction. But in this second function Wisdom avails itself primarily of the Law as a special divine gift, while the Spirit uses prophecy. This is a distinction with significant results.

Continuing our illustration of this similarity of function, we note that in several incidents relating to the Exodus there has occurred a transfer of function from one agency to another. This transfer is made by the writer of the Wisdom of Solomon, who tells us that Wisdom protected Joseph in Egypt and finally brought him to honor. In Genesis we are told that the Pharaoh recognized the presence of Divine Spirit in Joseph (Wisd. of Sol. 10:13; Gen. 41:38). This late interpreter of Hebrew history also tells us that the Divine

---

[3] *Der Geist Gottes und die verwandten Erscheinungen im Alten Testament und im anschliessenden Judentum* (Tübingen: J. C. B. Mohr, 1910), p. 186.

Wisdom had delivered the nation from slavery by entering the life of Moses and through him withstanding the tyrant, though in Isaiah we are told that God had put his Spirit in Moses to prepare him to lead the Exodus (Wisd. of Sol. 10:15 f.; Isa. 63:11). Pseudo-Solomon says that Wisdom guided Israel along the desert route, becoming for them a shelter by day and a flame of fire by night—a function also assigned to the Spirit elsewhere (10:17; Isa. 63:14; Hag. 2:5). In the latter account Wisdom led Israel across the Red Sea, though Exodus says that God piled up the water "by the breath of his nostrils" (10:18 f.; Exod. 15:18). The Wisdom of Solomon teaches that Wisdom, by means of a prophet, taught Israel God's providence and election through discipline in the desert. Thus, incidentally, Wisdom becomes the basis of prophetic capacity; but elsewhere the Spirit of Yahweh is the source of leadership, instruction, and enlightenment. The Wisdom of Solomon sets out deliberately to re-write all early history, beginning with Adam, in favor of Wisdom. In Isa. 63:11–14, much of this same activity had been assigned directly to God.

The Wisdom of Solomon also transfers to Wisdom the role formerly played by the Spirit in the special capacity of judges, leaders, and kings. The work is addressed to kings and proclaims that they reign by Divine Wisdom and that to rule forever they must pay heed to Wisdom (6:9; 8:13). The writer was undoubtedly aware that, throughout all Hebrew history, leaders had supposedly received special endowments of the Spirit. This was true both of Moses and of the elders who assisted him. The ceremony of the laying-on of hands, by which the impartation of the gift of spirit was symbolized in the consecration of kings and priests, had its origin in a grossly materialistic conception of spirit. Wisdom in rule, the gift of prophecy, prowess in battle—all these were transmitted by the gift of spirit to the leaders and rulers of the Hebrew nation. His possession of spirit made a ruler sacrosanct. Physically to harm "the Lord's annointed" was more than an insult to human royalty; it was an affront to God. The curious metaphor in the Book of Lamentations, which describes the king as "the breath of our nostrils," may derive from the accepted belief that the king possessed a special gift of the Divine Spirit (4:20). All the functions of political and spiritual leadership formerly assigned to Spirit Pseudo-Solomon assigns to Wisdom, "the holy Spirit of instruction" (1:7; 9:17).

As an eschatological gift for the future age, the Divine Spirit and Wisdom also play the same role. Those who despaired of wisdom in this age expected its presence in the golden age of the future (En. 5:8; 48:1; 49:1, 3; II Bar. 44:14). In like manner the possession of the Divine Spirit in the age to come is taught by writers of all types of eschatological thinking: the apocalyptic school, those who foresaw a less cataclysmic establishment of Israel in temporal glory, and those whose hopes are chiefly fixed upon the immortality of the soul. The Divine Spirit will operate in judgment and destruction to rid the nation of its impurities. In a reconstructed Israel a divinely appointed Messiah will possess the Spirit which is Wisdom itself (Isa. 11:12). God himself will be a spirit of justice among the people, teaching them right judgment and understanding, and in that age of righteousness, plenty, and peace even the dreary steppe will blossom. This will all be initiated by the gift of the Divine Spirit from on high (Isa. 28:6; Ezek. 11:19).

The second part of the Book of Isaiah carries the same conviction. The re-establishment is brought about and maintained in its great purpose by the operation of the Spirit upon the people (42:1; 44:3). The prophet and Cyrus, who are the heralds of the new era, the coming golden age, themselves have this Spirit (48:1; 61:1–3). Zerubbabel, who lays its foundations, is assured of the Spirit's operation in behalf of his projects, though in the First Book of Esdras he is personally assigned the gift of Divine Wisdom (4:59 f.). As the process develops, there is a constantly greater differentiation in the nature of the gifts of the Spirit, corresponding to the type of people to whom it is granted and the functions that they perform. The spirit of power, of understanding, of judgment and justice, the spirit of wisdom, and the spirit of prophecy—all are illustrations of this differentiation. Prophet, sage, and lawgiver all receive their special gift of the Spirit. And all the special aspects of it are brought together and poured out upon the single personality of the Messiah, who is the central figure of the new age.

In apocalyptic circles, where the new age is conceived in more transcendental terms, the special gift of the Spirit is likewise recognized. The saints will receive it; they will eat of the tree of life and possess the spirit of holiness; grace will be theirs, the gift of the Messiah upon them (Test. Lev. 18:11; Test. Juda 24:2 f.; En. 61:11). This gift will be the "spirit of the fear of the Lord"; that is, the Spirit will teach men their dependence upon God.

This dependence and transcendence reduces the element of human initiative, freedom, and responsibility, and for this reason the more conservative Pharisaic circles were always afraid of apocalypticism. Yet freedom and responsibility are never wholly lost; the tension between transcendence and freedom is as real for the order of grace as for the order of creation. As in the case of Wisdom, the special gift of grace that the Spirit is comes only to pious and holy men (Dan. 9:23; En. 51:1; IV Ezra 13:53-55; II Bar. 38:4). The only change is that the balance is in favor of grace rather than of nature.

How has this interrelationship of Wisdom and Spirit affected the former as an agency of, and as an index to, the conception of revelation held by those who employed it? Divine Spirit did not become identified with the Mosaic Code or with any other material object to which religion ascribed an eternal and transcendent sanctity. It came to earth in living human experience, heightening the individual capacity and insight of those who received it, and made men prophets and leaders. Thus, even though it was a special grace, it centered in life and was able to remain contemporaneous with the world into which it came.

This contemporaneity was impossible for Divine Wisdom so long as it was identified only with the Law; for, as we saw earlier, the Law lay to a large extent beyond human criticism; and with the passage of time it lay more and more outside of contemporary human experience. Therefore, by becoming identified with the Divine Spirit, as well as with the Law, Divine Wisdom received a new lease of life as an agency of revelation and as an instrument for its reception.

Thus, by interpreting the concept of Divine Wisdom as Spirit, the Wisdom of Solomon rendered inestimable service to the former; and, by transferring the functions of the Spirit to Wisdom, by making Wisdom the source of prophecy, and by affirming that Divine Wisdom came directly into human consciousness and experience, it assured to Divine Wisdom the same capacity of contemporaneity that was enjoyed by Spirit. The "Inspired Reason" of the Fourth Book of Maccabees must probably share this credit. This direct reception of Wisdom by living personalities had indeed been hinted at in Proverbs, chapters 1-9, and in Ben Sira; but in these and in other later wisdom writings the idea was obscured by the almost exclusive identification of Wisdom with the material Law. It remained for the Wisdom of Solomon to restore a dynamic vitality to Divine Wisdom by centering it fully in human consciousness and experience.

Both Wisdom and the Spirit had become symbols of special grace, and for both the rewards of faith lay beyond empirical verification. But, until the Wisdom concept became fully identified in function with that of Spirit, it lacked the latter's capability of receiving grace contemporaneously with the situation in which it was needed, and it also lacked the capability of evaluating it—to whatever extent grace can be evaluated—in the light of the contemporary situations in which it must be applied. As a man of the Spirit the prophet was not so independent as the early sage. He did not limit himself to natural human endowments in obtaining knowledge of the way of God but invoked the divine initiative. However, he retained an immediacy of grace in life and a creativity of spirit that could not be maintained by the sages, when they began to identify the divine initiative with a material code that was never contemporaneous.

When in the Wisdom of Solomon Divine Wisdom also appears as a spirit "passing into holy souls" and making them "friends of God and prophets," this agency and gift of grace could likewise remain always fluid and centered in living human experience. This may help to explain why, in the fresh creative outburst of the Jewish religious tradition represented by the New Testament, Wisdom identified as Law does not reappear, but Wisdom identified as Spirit does (I Cor. 12:8; Acts 6:10; Gal. 3:2). And the Spirit in which Divine Wisdom appears in the New Testament is likewise identified as a living, human personality with whom Wisdom is also equated (I Cor. 1:24, 30; II Cor. 3:17; Col. 2:3).

How ideas of revelation in the New Testament were affected by the equation of Wisdom and Spirit in the period preceding and what moral the whole history of the Hebrew wisdom movement offers those who struggle with the tension between nature and grace or those to whom both tangible authority and contemporaneity and freedom beckon alluringly are pertinent and challenging questions that go beyond our compass.

CHAPTER VI

CONCLUSION

HISTORICAL Christianity has normally adhered to the belief that ultimate reality is known through a special grace. It has not placed sole reliance on natural faculties and undirected human discovery as the instruments for the acquisition of knowledge about God; neither has it felt that the historical process as a whole is the arena in which the truth about existence is discernible. Consequently, there has always been a specific and particular reference or event in history which Christianity has considered of peculiar and final significance for a true understanding of God and of his way with men. This reference has been the life and career of Jesus; he has been the norm by which Christians measure all ideas about ultimate reality.

But Jesus is no longer empirically present in history. Hence the reference must be made to some medium that gives an authoritative account of him. During Christian history either the Bible or an institutional church has been commonly designated as the authoritative medium. Only sporadically and occasionally, it seems, has the Divine Spirit served as the instrument to mediate the true meaning of the life and career of Jesus and about the nature of existence.

The Christian story offers a rather close parallel to the Old Testament in this. The Israelites also considered particular events in history definitive for the true understanding of the nature of existence. For them God had revealed himself in such events as the Exodus, the sealing of the national covenant, and the establishment of the·nation in Palestine. The Law and the priests were normally expected to give authoritative interpretation of these particular historical events in which God was believed to have revealed himself. There were exceptions to this general rule. The prophets spoke with the authority of a personal conviction, which they considered a special gift immediately granted to them. The early sages rejected all ideas of a special historical reference as necessary to a true understanding of God. And the later wisdom movement exchanged the Law for the Divine Spirit as the peculiar organ of revelation.

Early Christianity was tutored in no small measure by these later stages of the wisdom movement, and it also seems to have fixed upon the Divine Spirit as the instrument for the interpretation of that peculiar historical event which it held definitive for a true understanding of God. So the Divine Spirit is declared to be the Spirit of Jesus, to indicate that it delivers the truth about him. This Spirit was felt to be an individual possession, enabling those who had it to speak with authority; so Paul used to settle arguments by an appeal to his possession of the Spirit. On the other hand, individuals who enjoyed this authoritative guide were also urged to test their personal convictions by the consciousness of the Christian fellowship as a whole. Indeed, the Spirit was also conceived as the possession of the entire fellowship.

In the earliest period of the Christian movement there was no clearly defined authoritative book or institution that could serve as the instrument for the interpretation of the divine revelation. But that alone hardly explains the acceptance of the authority of the Spirit in this function. In every subsequent creative period of the Christian movement the center of authority has been immediate, within the living experience of individuals in community, which has enabled men to give ventilation to new insights and encouraged them to throw off the shackles of fixed interpretations that were outworn or had lost all meaning. Luther, Fox, Wesley, and many others were nourished by this inner light of the Spirit that made them "speak with authority"—they had a living Word, a Divine Wisdom.

It is, nevertheless, true that Christians, for the most part, have never for long looked upon the Spirit as the final norm for the human soul in its search for truth. When a creative wave had spent itself, the final norm for thought and action receded from the immediacy of individual and group experience and found its rest in an institution with its system or in the literal book and the officially accepted statements about it. It was quite likely, of course, that both institution and book were modified in meaning and demand by the new insights which the creative period had uncovered. The fruits of the ventures of faith in one generation commonly become the inviolable boundaries of the next. During the comparatively long intermissions between creative outbursts, the church, instead of serving as a field in which the Spirit can work effectively, seeks to prevent the Spirit from stirring up the souls of men. Rather than letting the book serve as a tutor to bring men to new truth, it is conceived as a final statement that makes further thought superfluous. The role of the Spirit subsides; it simply operates to make men recognize the external authorities.

In the light of its history as a concept and the role it

played in the founding of Christianity, this neglect of the Divine Spirit by Christians seem strange; yet there are considerations that serve to explain it. The Spirit's role is in the intimacy of individual human experience. Thus it puts a severe test upon the urge to unity that concerns Christians; for it stresses freedom. Only a voluntary readiness of those guided by the Spirit to subject their convictions to a group examination makes it possible for people to live as with one will under its guidance. The bond of love, which should make men bring their convictions under the subjection of the authority of the Spirit over the fellowship, is usually too feebly developed in the mass of people whom the Christian institutions seek to hold together to serve as a real force for unity

There is another difficulty that has often made Christianity shy of the Spirit as the final authoritative medium of its historic revelation. This has been the fear that by appealing to the immediacy of human experience and conviction, even within the fellowship, it would be difficult to keep sight of the peculiar character of the Christian revelation. The holiness of the faith, it is felt, can be better protected by more tangible means. Christianity has always wanted to claim the masses; and instinctively it has usually known that the masses whom it claimed seldom knew that "spiritual things must be spiritually discerned." Difficulties such as these should not be discounted. They remind us that not easily do we hold as our own "the freedom of the sons of God." Yet that freedom seems to demand the authority of the Spirit.

SELECTED BIBLIOGRAPHY

BARTON, GEORGE A. *The Book of Ecclesiastes.* "International Critical Commentary." New York: Charles Scribner's Sons, 1908.

BAUMGARTNER, WALTER. *Israelitische und altorientalische Weisheit.* Tübingen: J. C. B. Mohr, 1933.

BERTHOLET, ALFRED. *A History of Hebrew Civilization.* Translated by A. K. DALLAS. London: George C. Harrap & Co., 1926.

BOUSSET, WILHELM. *Die Religion des Judentums im späthellenistischen Zeitalter.* Edited by HUGO GRESSMANN. Tübingen: J. C. B. Mohr, 1926.

CHARLES, R. H. *The Apocrypha and Pseudepigrapha of the Old Testament in English.* 2 vols. Oxford: Clarendon Press, 1913.

CHEYNE, T. K. *Job and Solomon; or the Wisdom of the Old Testament.* New York: Whittaker, 1887.

CONRAD, LUDWIG. *Die religiösen und sittlichen Anschauungen der alttestamentlichen Apokryphen und Pseudepigraphen.* Gütersloh: Bartlesmann, 1907.

DAVIDSON, ANDREW BRUCE. *The Book of Job.* Cambridge: At the University Press, 1899.

DILLON, E. J. *The Skeptics of the Old Testament: Job, Koheleth, Agur.* London: Isbister & Co., Ltd., 1895.

DRIVER, S. R., and GRAY, G. B. *The Book of Job: A Critical and Exegetical Commentary.* 2 vols. "International Critical Commentary." New York: Charles Scribner's Sons, 1921.

DUESBERG, HILAIRE. *Les Scribes inspirées: introduction aux livres sapientiaux de la Bible: Job, l'Ecclésiaste, l'Ecclésiastique—la sagesse.* Paris: Desclée de Brouwer, 1939.

DUPONT-SOMMER, ANDRÉ. *Le quatrième livre des Machabées; introduction, traduction, et notes.* Paris: Libraire ancienne Honoré Champion, 1939.

EBERHARTER, ANDREAS. *Das Buch Jesus Sirach, oder Ecclesiasticus, übersetzt und erklärt.* Bonn: Peter Hanstein, 1925.

123

EICHRODT, WALTHER. *Theologie des Alten Testaments.* 3 vols. Leipzig: J. C. Hinrichs, 1933–39.

EISSFELDT, OTTO. *Weisheit Salomos.* "Handbuch zum Alten Testament." Tübingen: Johannes Fichtner, 1938.

ERMAN, ADOLPH. *The Literature of the Ancient Egyptians: Poems, Narratives, and Manuals of Instruction from the Third and Second Millennia B.C.* Translated into English by AYLWARD M. BLACKMAN. London: Methuen & Co., 1927.

FAIRWEATHER, WILLIAM. *Background of the Gospels.* Edinburgh: T. and T. Clark, 1908.

FICHTNER, JOHANNES. *Die altorientalische Weisheit in ihr israelitischjüdischen Ausprägung: Eine Studie zur Nationalisierung der Weisheit in Israel.* Giessen: A. Töpelmann, 1933.

———. *Weisheit Salomos.* Tübingen: J. C. B. Mohr, 1938.

GEMSER, BEREND. *Sprüche Salomos.* Tübingen: J. C. B. Mohr, 1937.

GREGG, JOHN A. F. *The Wisdom of Solomon.* Cambridge: At the University Press, 1912.

GRESSMANN, HUGO. *Israels Sprüchenweisheit im Zusammenhang der Weltliteratur.* Berlin: Karl Curtius, 1925.

GRIFFITH, FRANCIS L. "The Teaching of Amenophis, the Son of Kanekht," *Journal of Egyptian Archeology,* XII (1926), 196 ff.

HEMPEL, JOHANNES. *Althebräische Literatur und ihre hellenistischjüdisches Nachleben.* Wildpark-Potsdam: Akademische Verlag Gesellschaft, 1930.

HERTZBERG, HANS W. *Der Prediger, übersetzt und erklärt.* Leipzig: A. Deichertsche Verlag D. Werner Scholl, 1932.

HUMBERT, PAUL. *Recherches sur les sources égyptiennes de la littérature sapientale d'Israel.* Neuchatel: Secrétariat de l'Université, 1929.

JASTROW, MORRIS. *A Gentle Cynic (Koheleth).* Philadelphia: J. B. Lippincott Co., 1919.

KÖBERLE, JUSTUS. *Natur und Geist nach der Auffassung des Alten Testaments.* München: Oskar Beck, 1901.

LA MORTE, ANDRÉ. *Le Livre de Qohéleth: étude critique et philosophique de l'Ecclésiaste.* Paris: Libraire Fischbacher, 1932.

LANGDON, STEPHEN. *Babylonian Wisdom.* London: Luzac & Co., 1923.

MACDONALD, DUNCAN B. *The Hebrew Philosophical Genius: A Vindication.* Princeton: Princeton University Press, 1936.

MEINHOLD, JOHANNES. *Die Weisheit Israels in Sprüche, Sage, und Dichtung.* Leipzig: Quelle & Meyer, 1908.

OESTERLEY, WILLIAM OSCAR EMIL. *An Introduction to the Books of the Apocrypha.* New York: Macmillan Co., 1925.

PEDERSEN, JOHANNES. *Israel: Its Life and Culture.* Oxford: Humphrey Milford, University Press, 1926.

PFEIFFER, ROBERT H. *Introduction to the Old Testament.* New York: Harper & Bros., 1941.

PODECHARD, ÉMILE. *L'Ecclésiaste.* Paris: Libraire Victor Le Coffre, 1912.

RANKIN, O. S. *Israel's Wisdom Literature: Its Bearing on Theology and the History of Religion.* Edinburgh: T. and T. Clark, 1936.

RANSTON, H. *The Old Testament Wisdom Books and Their Teaching.* London: Epworth Press, 1930.

REES, T. H. *The Holy Spirit in Thought and Experience.* New York: Charles Scribner's Sons, 1915.

SCHECHTER, SOLOMON. *Some Aspects of Rabbinic Theology.* New York: Macmillan Co., 1909.

SCHÜTZ, RODOLPHE. *Les Idées eschatologiques du livre de la sagesse.* Strasbourg: Imprimé par la première imprimérie Croat S. A. à Asijeh, Yougoslavie, 1936.

TOY, CRAWFORD H. *The Book of Proverbs: A Critical and Exegetical Commentary.* "International Critical Commentary." New York: Charles Scribner's Sons, 1908.

VOLZ, PAUL. *Der Geist Gottes und die Verwandten.* Tübingen: J. C. B. Mohr, 1910.

WOOD, IRVING F. *The Spirit of God in Biblical Literature.* New York: A. C. Armstrong & Son, 1904.

WÜTZ, FRANZ. *Das Buch Hiob.* Stuttgart: W. Kohlhammer, 1939.

INDEX

Alexandria, 28
Apocalyptic, 114 ff.

Babylon, Wisdom Literature of, 5
Ben Sira, exalts national tradition, 33

Caprice, 49
Causse, Antonin, 49
Cheyne, T. K., 59
Commerce, 2

Deuteronomy: eschatology, 50; view of history, 50
Divine initiative, 72 f., 82, 90
Divine names, 21 f.
Divine transcendence, 75 f., 89, 98
Duesberg, Hilaire, 48

Egypt: in Palestine, 3; Wisdom Literature of, 4 f.
Election, 34

Faith, 75; empirical verification of, 91; and reason, 96
"Fear of Yahweh," 71
Fichtner, Johannes, 21 f., 32, 37
Fools, 59 f., 86 f.
Free will, 65

Gemser, B., 6
God: his mercy, 26, 34 f.; his moral nature, 47 f.; his purposive character, 25 f.; man's Creator, 74
Grace, v, 75, 90 f., 116, 119
Gressmann, Hugo, 7
Gunkel, Hermann, theory of secular wisdom, 68 ff.

Hypostasis, 91

Individualism, 51 ff.
Israel, Wisdom Literature of, 5 f.

Josephus, 29

Koran, 29, 109

Law: coeternal with Wisdom, 38; core of national heritage, 30; normative, 32
Lods, Adolphe, 109

Man, 72, 79 f.
Messiah, 115
Mohammed, 108 f.
Moses, 113 f.

Nature, v, 90

Pfeiffer, Robert H., 6
Pirke Aboth, 46
Probation, 53
Prophets, 49 ff.
Providence, 15, 35

Rankin, O. S., 58, 78
Ras Shamra, 1
Religion, national, 19, 23
Revelation, vi, 97, 99, 116
Reward: eudaemonistic, 57 ff.; for individuals, 53; in prophets, 48 ff.; questioned by Job and Ecclesiastes, 76 ff.
Righteous, the, 69 f.

Sages: reject conversion, 63 f.; role of, 9 f.
Schechter, Solomon, 61
Spirit: equated with Wisdom, 104 ff.; nature of, 100 ff.; as power, 100
Synergism, 96 f.

127